The Ultimate
Field Guide to the U.S. Economy

The Ultimate
Field Guide to the U. S. Economy

A Compact and Irreverent Guide to
Economic Life in America

James Heintz, Nancy Folbre, and The Center for Popular Economics
with
The National Priorities Project *and* **United for a Fair Economy**

The New Press, New York

Grateful acknowledgment is made to the following for permission to reprint previously published material: The Art Institute of Chicago, Mike Constable, Norman Dog, Mike Konopacki, Peter Hannan, Nicole Hollander, Gary Huck, Barrie Maguire, Richard Mock, Oliphant, Ted Rall, Howard Saunders, Mike Thompson, Tom Toles, Tom Tomorrow, Dan Wassermann, and Matt Wuerker.

Library of Congress Cataloging-in-Publication Data
The ultimate field guide to the U.S. economy : a compact and irreverent guide to
economic life in America / James Heintz ... [et al.].
          p. cm.
Rev. ed. of: Field Guide to the U.S. economy / Nancy Folbre.
Includes bibliographical references.
ISBN 1-56584-578-1 (pbk.)
1. United States—Economic conditions. 2. Economic indicators—United States. I. Heintz, James.
II. Folbre, Nancy. Field Guide to the U.S. economy.
HC 103. F59 2000
330.973—dc21   99–048804

Published in the United States by The New Press, New York
Distributed by W. W. Norton & Company, Inc., New York

The New Press was established in 1990 as a nonprofit alternative to the large, commercial publishing houses currently dominating the book publishing industry. The New Press operates in the public interest rather than for private gain, and is committed to publishing, in innovative ways, works of educational, cultural, and community value that are often deemed insufficiently profitable.

Book design by Robert Dworak
Production management by Fran Forte
www.thenewpress.com
Printed in Canada

9 8 7 6 5 4 3 2 1

Contents

Chapter 10: The Global Economy ... 174

Toolkit ... 194

Glossary ... 207

Sources ... 213

Acknowledgments

As ever, our efforts at revising and updating the Field Guide were motivated by the ongoing teaching needs of the Center for Popular Economics and other economic literacy projects, including the National Priorities Project and United for a Fair Economy. Many individuals contributed in one way or another, digging up numbers, commenting on drafts, or suggesting artwork.

This version has been even more collaborative than usual. Chuck Collins, Chris Hartman, and other staff of United for a Fair Economy provided much of the material for Chapter 1. Likewise, Paul Newlin and Laura Beavers of the National Priorities Project made substantial contributions to Chapter 5. Jim Westrich helped design and execute Chapter 7, while Hector Saez put together many of the changes to Chapter 8. Elissa Braunstein, James Crotty, Gerald Epstein, and Robert Pollin offered useful input for Chapters 9 and 10. In addition to serving as book designer and layout maestro, Robert Dworak orchestrated the entire data collection and file management process. Bill Weye provided general research assistance.

Much of the original artwork for this version was enthusiastically provided by R. Jay Magill. We remain grateful to Nicholas Blechman (a.k.a. Knickerbocker) and Russell Christian for many spot illustrations. Special thanks to the many cartoonists who donated all or a substantial portion of their permission fees: Nicole Hollander, Gary Huck, Mike Konopacki, Richard Mock, Tom Tomorrow, Dan Wasserman, and Matt Wuerker.

Susan Stinson's relentless enthusiasm and fundraising got us started and kept us going. Elissa Braunstein, Helen Johnson, and Tom Masterson helped out us directly, as well as indirectly by keeping the Center for Popular Economics going. Participants at the 1998 Summer Institute gave advice and encouragement. As usual, André Schiffrin, Ellen Reeves, Fran Forte, and Hall Smyth of the New Press offered excellent guidance.

The Bottom Line

If there were just one bottom line, the U.S. economy would be easier to understand. We could pretend that it was just one big checking account, and we could look at our monthly statement to see how we were doing. We could see who made the deposits and who made the withdrawals and figure out who got what and why. It's not so simple because an economy is more than a set of accounts: It's a system of production. People put their labor, their talents, and a little bit of their soul into it and take their livelihood out of it. Some people get rich, some get poor; sometimes the overall economy grows, sometimes it falters. Not even the best economists in the world understand exactly how it works.

But most people want to know more about it, if only because they're worried about the bottom line in their own checkbooks. The stock market is booming, but the real wages of the typical U.S. worker are no higher now than in 1970. New medical technologies abound, but many families can't afford health insurance. The unemployment rate is low, but even experienced professionals and managers remain susceptible to downsizing. People are also worried about the larger economic trends affecting their communities, their country, and their world: global financial crises, the movement of U.S. corporations abroad, growing income inequality, high levels of child poverty, and the threat of major environmental problems. Alas, most politicians remain preoccupied with sex, war, and tax cuts—not to mention re-election.

Those who know a great deal about the U.S. economy are often exceedingly fond of it. Economic experts are far more likely to extol the virtues of the system than to criticize it.

Prevailing orthodoxy holds that the economy does not need critics, watchdogs, or gadflies of any sort and, indeed, works much better without them. Typical economics courses confine their attention to the theory of competitive markets and treat the economy as a self-regulating system. Even when they address issues of public policy, economists often teach students that there is an inevitable trade-off between equity and efficiency. The message, in ordinary language, is that social justice is just too expensive.

Some economists (like us) disagree. We believe that economic power in the U.S. is unevenly distributed and easily abused, that current economic policies are inefficient as well as unfair. We also believe that good citizens should be good critics, that controversy and debate over economic issues are central to the democratic process. This book compiles useful information for non-economists (as well as students and teachers) who want to know more about the U.S. economy. The facts and figures we highlight reflect our personal values and our political concerns. But we stop short of developing any one interpretation of U.S. economic trends or advocating any particular social policies. Our aim here is not to persuade but to inform and provoke, enlighten and enliven economic debate.

The Ultimate Field Guide to the U.S. Economy is the third version we have published, and one which we plan to update on the Web (www.fguide.org). It is designed to serve as an accessible, concise reference for answering specific questions as well as an informative overview of the U.S. economy. Each page stands alone as a description of an economic fact or trend but also fits into a chapter that systematically covers a particular topic. You might want to read the book from cover to cover. More likely, you might want to scan the table of contents, pick a page title that interests you, and follow your nose. Ten chapters of charts are followed by a toolkit section, bibliographic sources for the charts, and a glossary. Each of the first four chapters explains the economic position and history of an important group of people: "Owners," "Workers," "Women," and "People of Color." Each of the following six chapters covers a particular area of concern: "Government," "Welfare and Education," "Health," "Environment," "Macroeconomics," and "The Global Economy." The later chapters, the last two in particular, use some technical terms that make them more difficult than the early chapters. But anyone who is curious and persistent enough to consult the Glossary should be able to figure them out.

Each chapter opens with a brief overview that ties its charts together around the main theme. The pages tend to progress from the more general to the more specific, providing a variety of types of information—descriptions of widely discussed trends, explanations of basic economic concepts, and occasionally, more speculative analysis of possibilities for change. While most of the charts trace one economic variable over time, some examine the relationship between important economic variables. Whenever feasible, we track historical data back to 1960.

The ten sections in the Toolkit are designed to help readers interpret and use economic statistics. They include reminders about how to read graphs and explanations of things like price indices and the poverty line. The Glossary provides clear, simple definitions of many technical terms.

This book has been shaped by its most immediate audience. For the past 20 years, the Center for Popular Economics has organized and taught workshops on economic issues for community organizers and activists. Our students constantly demanded more information, more explanation, more documentation. Every year, we added to a pile of classroom handouts; every year, we found it harder to keep our pile organized and up-to-date. In the summer of 1984, we took the initial step of transferring our handouts to computer files and began to experiment with computer-generated graphs. Our students loved the results. "Make it a book," they exclaimed, "but make it more fun." Their enthusiasm fanned our ambition to produce an illustrated guide to the U.S. economy.

The first edition was a big hit and was adopted for use in many classrooms across the country. Fans, friends, students, and colleagues soon began asking for updates. A second version, published in 1995, included a great deal of new material focusing on hot political issues. As 1998 rolled around we realized that the book needed to keep evolving. Mobilizing the energy of a new lead author and the assistance of the National Priorities Project and United for a Fair Economy, we produced this *Ultimate Field Guide*, chock-full of information for the next millennium.

What you have here represents our commitment to a kind of economics that is popular in the best sense of the word—it's aimed at ordinary people. Put these facts and figures to good use. "Never doubt," wrote anthropologist Margaret Mead, "that a small group of thoughtful, committed citizens can change the world. Indeed, it is the only thing that ever has."

Chapter 1 **Owners**

Russell Christian

From Easy Street to Skid Row, the haves and have-nots coexist in towns across America. But who actually owns what in the United States? This chapter looks at the distribution of family wealth and the structure of corporate power.

Them that's got shall get. The story of wealth in America is one of silver spoons and stock market booms. Individuals compete against each other in a capitalist economy, their success partly determined by the wealth they bring with them to the market. Some people bring nothing but their need for work. Others bring expensive skills or financial assets; when they leave, they often take home even more.

Chart 1.1 shows that the richest 10% of all families own 83% of the financial wealth in America. The bottom 80% only get 8%. These inequalities are growing greater. As Chart 1.2 points out, the wealthiest 1% of households increased their portion of the pie over the past decade.

While many families own a bit of wealth, the richest claim the lion's share. Chart 1.3 shows that the top 10% own over 90% of all business equity. Those who think that the playing field has leveled in the late 20th century should check out Chart 1.4. In 1995, the financial wealth of white families, on average, was over 90 times that of African-American households.

Chart 1.5 lists the six wealthiest individuals and families in the world along with an estimate of their fortunes. Chart 1.6 puts this vast store of wealth into perspective, calculating what it could purchase if directed towards basic schooling, reproductive care for women, and health services.

Only a minority of billionaires acquired their riches themselves. Chart 1.6 shows where the richest Americans got their money. Much of it was inherited. Others simply had the good luck to head up a major corporation. Chart 1.7 examines the pay of Chief Executive Officers (CEOs) relative to an average production worker.

Wealth and income are closely related, but not identical. Chart 1.9 shows the distribution of income among different families in the United States, while Chart 1.10 indicates where that income comes from. For most, the primary source of income is a job, not an investment portfolio.

Wealth bestows more than a high standard of living. Often political power comes up for sale. Chart 1.11 details the relative size of contributions that business, labor, and single-issue organizations make to political action committees. Elections are subject to influence. Chart 1.12 shows the difference in spending between winners and losers of congressional campaigns. Control over the media, another means of buying power, is illustrated in Chart 1.13.

Corporations consolidate their influence by combining forces. Chart 1.14 lists some of the biggest recent mergers. As Chart 1.15 shows, the size of many multinational businesses today makes the economies of entire countries look puny. While the concentration of wealth in the United States might feel overwhelming, some inroads have been made. Chart 1.16 looks at ways in which workers can acquire shares of the firms they work for.

1.1 Who Owns How Much?

"The rich are different from you and me," said F. Scott Fitzgerald. "Yes," replied Ernest Hemingway. "They have more money." More specifically, they have more wealth, an accumulation of money and other assets.

In the U.S., a small fraction of the people control most of the wealth. In 1997, the richest tenth of households owned 83% of the country's financial assets. The bottom four-fifths owned only 8%.

It's nice to be wealthy: income arrives whether or not you work. A nice cushion protects you from the ups and downs of the business cycle.

If we were to sketch a portrait of the richest households in America, what would it look like? In 1995, of the top 1% of wealth-holders, 95% were white, 72% were between 45 and 74, 88% reported good to excellent health, and about 70% had been to college.

r. jay magill

Distribution of financial wealth in 1997 (by groups of households)

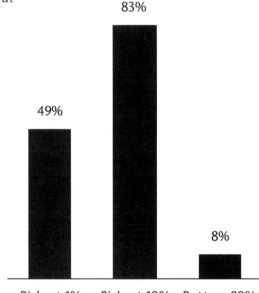

	49%	83%	8%
	Richest 1%	Richest 10%	Bottom 80%

1.2 Very Rich, Getting Richer

If thou hast, thou shalt receive. At least, that's been the rule in the U.S. for years. In 1983, the richest 1% of households owned 43% of the country's financial wealth. By 1997, they had 49%. With the crème de la crème claiming a bigger piece of the pie, there's less for everyone else. The share of the bottom 90% of households dropped from 20% to 17% over the same period.

In the 1970s, the distribution of wealth in America didn't look much different from the inequalities in other industrialized countries. But by the 1980s, the U.S. had become the most unequal.

In recent years, the run-up in the stock market has made the rich even richer. Business assets, financial securities, and mutual funds account for over 67% of the wealth of the top 1%. Less wealthy households haven't shared in the boom to the same extent. The wealth they have, if any, is mostly tied up in their homes.

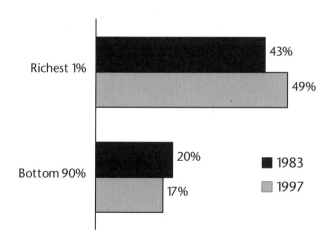

Share of total financial wealth (by groups of households)

Richest 1%: 43% (1983), 49% (1997)

Bottom 90%: 20% (1983), 17% (1997)

■ 1983
▨ 1997

1.3 What the Wealthy Own

It's not if you own, it's how much you own. While 41% of all households held some stock in 1995, most didn't have very much. The richest 10% of households controlled 88% of all stocks, 92% of business equity, and 90% of financial securities.

The fact that stock ownership has recently become more common doesn't mean that financial wealth is distributed more evenly. Most of the wealth of the middle class is concentrated in houses and cars. The few stocks they own are often held indirectly in retirement and mutual funds.

Home ownership provides many families with some wealth; however, large mortgages reduce the net amount people actually own. In 1983, mortgage debt comprised 21 percent of the value of an average home, but jumped up to 36 percent by 1995.

Distribution of wealth in 1995, by households

The richest 1 percent held:
51 percent of all stocks and mutual funds
70 percent of all business equity
66 percent of all financial securities

The richest 10 percent held:
88 percent of all stocks and mutual funds
92 percent of all business equity
90 percent of all financial securities

1.4 The Color of Wealth

If a Ford Escort represents the average financial wealth of an African-American household, you would need a stretch limousine 300 yards long to show the average for a white household. In fact, for many African Americans, net wealth is negative; people owe more than they own.

Latino families don't have it any better. In 1995, their median net financial wealth was zero.

In times of stress, wealth makes a crucial difference. A sudden loss of income because of job loss, illness, or family breakup can mean poverty. When things get tough, white households use their wealth to keep their heads above water. With far fewer reserves, families of color are more likely to go under.

Wealth passed from generation to generation explains much of this disparity. In 1995, 24% of white households reported that they had received inheritances at some time: the average value was $115,000. Only 11% of African Americans had received inheritances, averaging $32,000.

Tom Tomorrow

Median financial wealth of households in 1995

African Americans $200

Whites $18,100

1.5 The Richest People in the World

Picture King Alsaud and the Sultan of Brunei downloading the latest version of Microsoft Internet Explorer so they can invest on the web, following advice from the book *Warren Buffet Speaks*. The six largest individual fortunes in the world would all be represented, collectively representing a total net worth of over $230 billion.

Rich people don't like anything to get between them and their money. The Department of Justice has been investigating unfair competitive practices at Microsoft, the source of three of the six top fortunes. Many communities have accused Wal-Mart, owned by one of America's richest families, the Waltons, of driving small local retailers out of business.

King Alsaud of Saudi Arabia and the Sultan of Brunei used a different approach. They got their money the old-fashioned way. They inherited it.

The six richest people in the world (by net worth) in 1999

Bill Gates, U.S.	$90 billion
Warren Edward Buffet, U.S.	$36 billion
Sultan Hassanal Bolkiah, Brunei	$30 billion
Paul Gardner Allen, U.S.	$30 billion
King Alsaud, Saudi Arabia	$28 billion
Steven Ballmer, U.S.	$20 billion

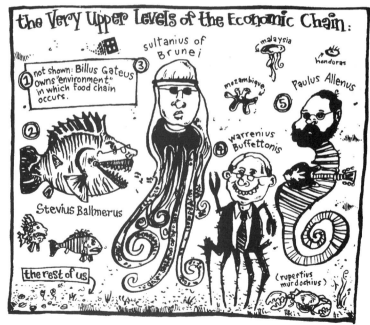

r. jay magill

1.6 Gross Inequalities

As the rich get richer, it becomes hard to imagine what the wealth of the ultra-rich actually means.

- The cost of providing basic education and health care, as well as adequate food and safe water for all the people of earth, is estimated to be $40 billion—less than the net worth of Bill Gates.

- The three richest people in the world have assets that exceed the combined GDP of the 48 poorest countries.

- The combined wealth of the 32 richest people exceeds the total GDP of South Asia.

- The wealth of the 225 richest people is equal to the annual incomes of the poorest 47 percent of the world's population (over 2.5 billion people).

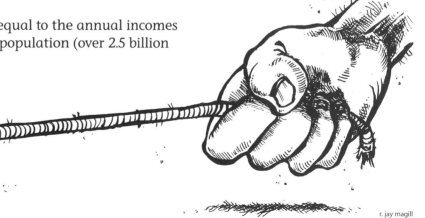

r. jay magill

1.7 Born on Third Base

How did the richest people in American get their money? Some started with very little and built up their fortunes. But many billionaires started out in life with millions. Scoring big was easy.

Each year *Forbes* magazine profiles the 400 wealthiest individuals in the U.S. In 1997, 42% of them inherited enough wealth to rank among the richest without doing anything else. Less than one-third of them started without inherited wealth.

For most people the American dream is just that—a dream. Most don't get a fair chance in the batter's box. While the total wealth of the richest 400 increased by 31% between 1996 and 1997, median weekly earnings for full-time non-supervisory workers grew only 4%.

How the *Forbes 400* began their fortunes

Parents did not have great wealth or own a business	31%
Family was upper-class but had less than $1 million, or received some start-up capital from a family member.	14%
Inherited a medium-size business, wealth of more than $1 million, or substantial startup capital.	7%
Inherited wealth in excess of $50 million or a large company.	6%
Inheritance alone was enough to qualify for the *400*.	42%

Nick Thorkelson

20

1.8 CEO Pay

A worker in the U.S. would have to work four and a half centuries just to earn what the average Chief Executive Officer (or CEO) gets in one year. In the future, it will probably take even longer. Between 1997 and 1998, production workers saw their earnings increase by 4% while CEOs got an average raise of 36%.

The best-paid employees are also owners. Much of the compensation CEOs get includes stock options—the ability to purchase company stock at favorable terms. For over 350 of the country's highest paid executives, stock options account for 72% of their pay packages. The benefits are enormous. When Disney chairman Michael Eisner exercised a fraction of his options in 1997, he earned over half a billion dollars.

Are CEOs worth it? Higher pay does not guarantee superior performance. In 1998, companies with the highest-paid executives didn't outperform other firms. Plus, CEOs overseas don't enjoy the same perks. In 1997, the packages of British CEOs amounted to only 24% of those of their American counterparts. This gap isn't likely to last long. Many European countries have already begun adopting American-style bonuses.

r. jay magill

Average production worker's pay compared to average CEO's pay in 1998

← Production worker: $22,976

Chief Executive Officer: $10,600,000

1.9 Scraping By

Many people live from paycheck to paycheck, year after year, without much to show for it. When income flows just cover the basic costs of living, building up even small amounts of wealth becomes impossible.

In 1997, the fifth of households with the smallest earnings scraped by with an average income of just $8,872. On the other side of the tracks, the top fifth enjoyed an average of $122,764. Things aren't getting any more equal. Between 1990 and 1997, income at the bottom virtually stagnated while the top fifth of earners got a 15% boost.

Income and wealth are related in two ways. People with high incomes can accumulate wealth, and those with wealth get income from the assets they own. But for most people outside this elite circle, income is just a means of surviving.

Richard Mock

Mean household income in 1997, by income group

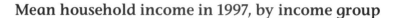

	Mean Income	% change from 1990
Highest fifth (above $71,500)	$122,764	14.7%
Fourth fifth ($46,001-$71,500)	$57,582	4.4%
Third fifth ($29,201-$46,000)	$37,177	1.7%
Second fifth ($15,401-$29,200)	$22,098	-0.2%
Lowest fifth (Below $15,400)	$8,872	0.4%

1.10 Who Gets Money From What?

Knickerbocker

Why does the evening news say so much more about stock prices than about wages? After all, most people get their income from work. The state of the labor market affects their lives much more directly than the stock market does.

In 1997, 71% of people over 15 years old received some kind of paycheck. Compare this with the number who got money from dividends: only 17%.

Social Security remains an important source of income for the elderly. In 1996, 91% of the elderly population received income from Social Security, while only 30% received income from private pensions.

Thanks to money in savings accounts, 54% of adults earned some interest in 1997. The average amount, however, was relatively small. Far fewer people got income from rents, royalties, estates, and trusts. Because many of these people only received small amounts, the average from these sources was also low.

Sources of personal income in 1997

	Percent	Mean Income
Wages and Salaries	71.0%	$28,415
Nonfarm self-employment	6.0%	$23,180
Social Security	19.7%	$8,359
Pensions	7.6%	$12,220
Interest	53.7%	$1,869
Dividends	17.2%	$2,883
Rents, Royalties, Estates, Trusts	6.6%	$4,316

1.11 The Price of Influence

Everyone knows that money talks, but in U.S. politics it hollers. Many individuals, corporations, and political action committees (PACs) gave money to Congressional campaigns in 1995-96. But business outspent everyone else by a large margin with a combined investment of over $450 million in its favored candidates.

Unions raised only 11% of that amount. Unlike individual firms, individual unions did not donate, keeping contributions relatively low. Other groups, including those focused on single issues such as gun rights, spent about $20 million more than organized labor did.

In 1997-98, the top contributions came from lawyers, retirement organizations, investors, realtors, and insurance companies. Tobacco interests contributed almost three times the amount that health services did, and the gambling industry spent 12 times more than environmental groups did.

Contributions to congressional campaigns, 1995-96 (in millions of $)

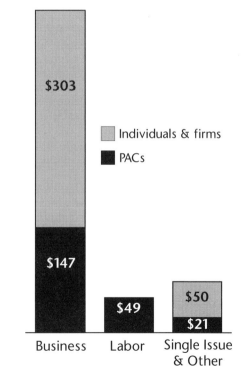

- Individuals & firms
- PACs

Business: $303 / $147
Labor: $49
Single Issue & Other: $50 / $21

1.12 Dollar Democracy

In American elections, you get what you pay for. In 1996, winners of seats in the House of Representatives spent more than twice as much as losers did. Winners in the Senate spent over $4.5 million on average, nearly 70% more than losers spent. With money playing such a decisive role, it's no wonder many registered voters don't turn out on election day.

Once in office, members of Congress can more easily attract private contributions, particularly if they sit on a high-stakes committee. The more powerful the committee, the larger the donations, and the better the chance of influencing public policy.

Enforcing the rules that control the financing of elections remains a problem. In 1974, the government established the Federal Election Commission to collect information and monitor behavior during national elections. Many state governments also set up watchdog agencies following the Watergate scandal. However, these organizations currently lack the power and resources to back up even the existing laws.

The system of private financing makes it difficult for candidates to win without backing from interest groups. Elected officials will remain beholden to those who put up the money until serious campaign reform is implemented and stringently enforced.

Tom Tomorrow

Average spending of winners and losers in congressional campaigns in 1996

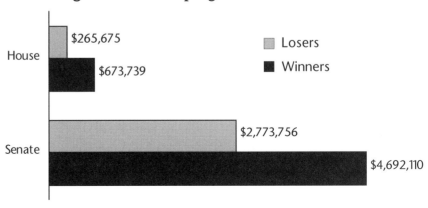

1.13 Controlling Media

You get home from work and turn on CNN to catch up with the news. During the commercials, you flip through *Time* and *Sports Illustrated*. After seeing what's on HBO, you decide to go out to a Warner Brother's movie. Your entire evening, quite possibly including your cable service and local cinema, would have been brought to you by one giant corporation: Time Warner.

Ownership of the media industry has become more concentrated. The two largest corporations, Time Warner and Disney, tripled in size over the past decade. As fewer firms own more, their profit margins will shape the news we get, the entertainment we enjoy, and the information we have access to.

In the 1980s and 1990s, many countries privatized and deregulated their national media systems, paving the way for the huge media companies to go global. The largest firms now have worldwide influence. While this development might displace local cultural activities, it provides travelers with some dubious comfort: no matter where you are in the world, you can find a familiar face just by flipping on the TV.

1.14 Mega-Mergers

The twilight years of the 20th century have witnessed the largest mergers in world history. The boom in U.S. financial markets created the financial resources for the consolidation of economic power. Increased competition and the drive to expand profits provided the incentives. The most notable mega-mergers include:

Exxon/Mobil: At the end of 1998, Exxon Corporation agreed to buy Mobil for $77.2 billion, forming the largest company in the U.S. Financial benefits of about $3 billion will come at the expense of the 9,000 employees who will lose their jobs in the consolidation.

Citicorp/Travelers: This $73 billion merger created the financial services behemoth Citigroup. The new giant, unbalanced by instability in financial markets, ended 1998 with an announcement of 10,400 job cuts.

BankAmerica/NationsBank: In mid-1998, the Federal Reserve and the Justice Department approved a $57 billion deal which produced the biggest depository bank in the U.S. Such mergers make the prospect of a banking crisis scary—BankAmerica has deposits almost ten times greater than the FDIC's entire fund.

Daimler-Benz/Chrysler: When Daimler-Benz purchased Chrysler for $40 billion, it was the largest merger in the history of the automobile industry. Competitive pressures from the new colossus have already provoked further concentration. In 1999, Ford snatched up Volvo for $6.5 billion.

TOLES © 1998 The Buffalo News. Reprinted with permission of the UNIVERSAL PRESS SYNDICATE. All rights reserved.

1.15 Multinational Goliaths

The size of today's giant corporations often dwarfs the economies of entire countries. In 1996, total sales of General Motors, Mitsubishi, and Wal-Mart exceeded the gross domestic products of Mozambique, Malaysia, and Ukraine. While U.S. foreign policy puts a big emphasis on democracy and human rights when dealing with small countries, the same concepts aren't applied to multinationals.

Multinationals have an enormous global reach. Because they operate across national boundaries, regulation proves difficult. Their ability to move from one country to another gives them an edge when striking deals with local communities and governments. If a multinational feels that labor laws or environmental codes are too restrictive, it can always threaten to leave.

World sales of selected multinationals and Gross National Product of selected countries in 1996 (in billions of $1996)

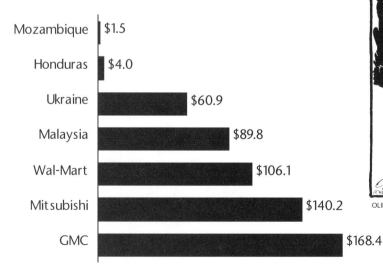

Mozambique	$1.5
Honduras	$4.0
Ukraine	$60.9
Malaysia	$89.8
Wal-Mart	$106.1
Mitsubishi	$140.2
GMC	$168.4

OLIPHANT ©1998 UNIVERSAL PRESS SYNDICATE. Reprinted with permission. All rights reserved.

28

1.16 Worker Owners

Looking for an alternative to the current concentration of wealth in the American economy? Worker ownership provides one potential answer. Increasingly, workers are buying shares in the companies for which they work. The National Center for Employee Ownership estimated that U.S. workers controlled about 8% of total corporate equity in 1997.

Many roads lead to greater worker ownership. Employee Stock Ownership Plans (ESOPs) establish a trust fund through which workers acquire new and existing company stock. 401(k) plans give workers tax incentives to invest for their retirement. Often companies match 401(k) investments with their own stock. And profit-sharing arrangements give workers a piece of the owners' income without actually transferring property.

Ownership is one thing, control another. In most cases, worker ownership remains too small to provide much influence over corporate strategies. Worker-owners often don't have full voting rights. Employees could end up sharing the risk of ownership without having any voice in governing the firm.

Employee ownership plans in 1998

Type of Plan	Number of Employees	Value of Assets
Employee Stock Ownership Plans (ESOPs) and stock bonus plans.	7.7 million	$400 billion
401(k) Plans primarily invested in employer stock and profit-sharing arrangements.	2 million	$250 billion

Chapter 2 **Workers**

Russell Christian

What kind of jobs do Americans have? Who gets the big bucks and who works for peanuts? And why can't some people find employment? This chapter looks at work in the United States, making connections between wages, unemployment, and income.

Women are increasing their overall hours of paid work, while men are decreasing theirs. Chart 2.1 documents trends in labor force participation by gender. Sectoral employment is also changing. Many manufacturing jobs have disappeared, replaced by rapid growth in service employment, documented in Chart 2.2. Many of these new jobs offer relatively low pay and sparse benefits.

How have hourly wages changed in the 1990s? Chart 2.3 tells the story. In spite of recent gains, inflation-adjusted wages remain well below their peak in the mid-1970s. A look at weekly earnings by race in Chart 2.4 shows that while all groups experienced a decline, African Americans and Latinos have been hurt the most over the past two decades. Young workers don't have much to look forward to either. Chart 2.5 points out that entry-level wages have fallen for both men and women.

Increases in the federal minimum wage have not been sufficient to combat inflation. Chart 2.6 tracks the ups and downs (mostly the latter) of the real minimum wage over nearly fifty years. Of course, paychecks don't tell the whole story. Benefits are also important. Once upon a time, employer contributions to pension plans and health insurance made up for declining pay. But as Chart 2.7 indicates, the era of generous benefits is over, and cutbacks are the new name of the game.

All these factors contribute to growing inequalities among workers. Chart 2.8 shows that the gap between the wages of the highest-paid and lowest-paid workers has grown. Many workers with families are slipping below the poverty line despite working full-time. Chart 2.9 provides information on the working poor and explains why full-time employment might not be an adequate remedy for low incomes. Chart 2.10 offers one possible solution—enact policies which pay workers a wage their families can live on.

Not all jobs are created equal. Many are part-time or temporary. Chart 2.11 shows the extent to which people are underemployed, making do with less than full-time work. Other people can't find jobs at all. Although unemployment rates have fallen recently, young people, African Americans, and Latinos still experience significant difficulties finding work. Chart 2.12 shows the variation across groups, while Chart 2.13 traces unemployment rates over time.

Downsizing has been hard on many workers. What happens to people who lose their jobs when corporations restructure? Look at Chart 2.14. Some remain unemployed for long periods, while others drop out of the labor force. Of those who do find new jobs, the majority are rehired at lower pay.

Historically, trade unions have been able to fight for workers' rights. They have improved the living standards of their members and, to some extent, those of workers in general. Although unions have discriminated in the past, Chart 2.15 shows the important roles women and people of color play in the modern labor movement. While union membership has been falling for years, Chart 2.16 points to signs that organized labor in America is gathering strength.

2.1 Who's in the Labor Force?

Knickerbocker

Women doing more paid work, men doing less. That was the trend from 1950 until recently. Now women's entrance into the paid labor force is leveling off.

Maybe people are just running out of time. Further increases in hours devoted to paid employment would mean even fewer hours for running errands and caring for family members. If women could convince men to take on more of these responsibilities, male and female labor force participation rates might eventually converge.

Declines in male labor force participation rates since 1950 don't reflect an increase in the number of househusbands. Many men have taken early retirement thanks to expanding social security benefits and, for those with good jobs, secure pensions. In addition, a large number of poorly educated men, discouraged by a lack of opportunities, have stopped looking for work.

U.S. labor force participation rates, 1950-98

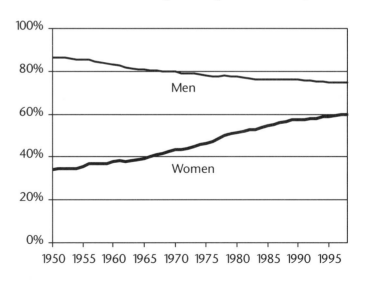

2.2 Bye-bye Factory Jobs

Between 1980 and 1997, the U.S. economy churned out an additional 32 million new jobs. Most of this growth was in the service sector. During this period, 1.6 million manufacturing jobs disappeared, despite the fact that real manufacturing output grew by over 66%.

Factory work has never been fun, but it once offered secure and relatively well-paying jobs to men and women who were willing to work hard. Not any more. Many have lost their jobs due to downsizing and plant closings. The drive to make U.S. manufacturing lean and mean has worked. Workers are so much more productive now that firms can make do with fewer of them.

While some service-sector jobs pay well, they often fail to match the pay and benefits of traditional factory jobs. Relatively unskilled work such as data entry, scanning groceries, and telemarketing pays poorly, offers few benefits, and often is limited to part-time hours.

In 1997, the average hourly compensation was $13.17 for a manufacturing job and $11.58 for a service job.

Russell Christian

Change in employment, by sector, 1980-97

51%

Services

-8%

Manufacturing

2.3 The Wage Treadmill

Many American workers are on a treadmill, running faster and faster without making progress. In the 1950's and 60's, when the U.S. economy grew, workers shared in the prosperity. However, in most years since the mid-70's, workers' hourly wages, adjusted for inflation, fell. This trend began to reverse itself in 1996, but real wages remain well below their 1973 peak.

Lower real wages mean that people must work harder just to maintain their standard of living. Much of this burden falls on the shoulders of women. Between 1979 and 1996, the average number of hours women worked on the job increased by 37%.

Lack of progress is particularly discouraging for those at the bottom. Many full-time workers don't earn enough to keep their families out of poverty.

Average hourly earnings, 1950-98
(private nonagricultural, nonsupervisory workers, in $1997)

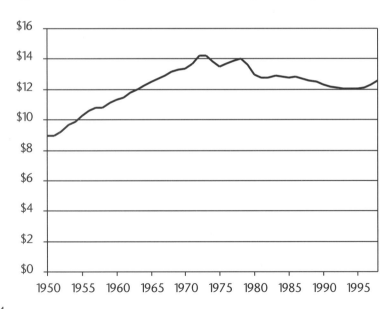

2.4 Skimpy Paychecks

Paying rent and buying groceries chews up more of a weekly paycheck than in the past.

While many people have compensated for low hourly earnings by working more, median weekly earnings of full-time workers have deteriorated since the 1970s.

Earnings can be measured in a variety of ways, but the take-home message remains pretty much the same. Both average hourly wages and weekly earnings are lower today than in 1973. Also, racial and ethnic differences in earnings have become more extreme in recent years.

The Census Bureau did not publish distinct statistics on African Americans and Latinos until 1979, making long-term comparisons difficult. But people of color narrowed the pay gap with whites between 1970 and 1978. After 1979, that gap increased.

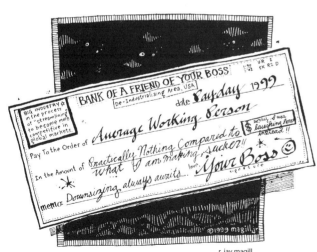

r. jay magill

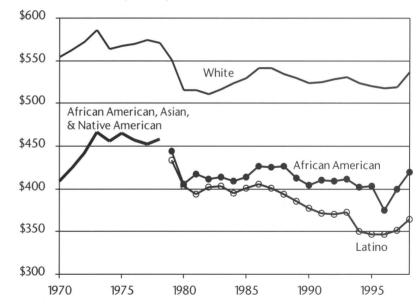

Median weekly earnings of full-time workers, 1970-98 ($1997)

35

2.5 Tough Luck, Kids

Think the American economy guarantees that each generation will start off with better opportunities today than in the past? Guess again. High school graduates finding a job for the first time in 1997 earned lower real hourly wages than they did in 1989.

More education doesn't solve the problem (though it may protect job seekers from even steeper declines). Among first-time job seekers with a college education, average real hourly wages dropped from $14.60 in 1989 to $13.65 in 1996 for men, and from $13.17 to $12.20 for women.

The gap between young women and young men has narrowed, but not because women are earning more. Men's entry-level wages have just fallen faster.

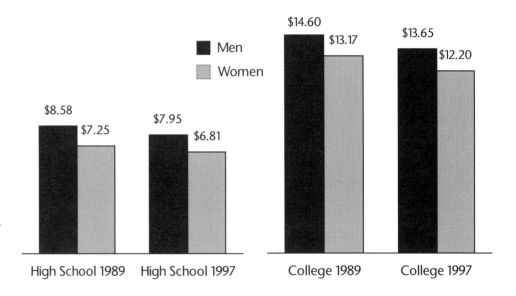

Hourly entry-level wages, by educational attainment ($1997)

Men
Women

$8.58 — High School 1989
$7.25 — High School 1989

$7.95 — High School 1997
$6.81 — High School 1997

$14.60 — College 1989
$13.17 — College 1989

$13.65 — College 1997
$12.20 — College 1997

2.6 The Minimal Minimum Wage

Minimum wages are supposed to set a basic standard of decency, but that standard has been slipping. Despite a recent increase of the national minimum wage to $5.15 an hour, its real value remains below what it was throughout the 1960s and 1970s.

In the 1950s and 1960s, Congress boosted the minimum wage several times, more than enough to compensate for inflation. But since 1968, when it peaked, its purchasing power has drifted down.

The low minimum wage means poverty for many families. At $5.15 an hour in 1999, a full-time worker brought home less than $11,000 a year, far below the poverty line established by the Census Bureau for a family of four.

Some economists argue that a higher minimum wage would discourage employers from hiring. Others emphasize that such dangers are small compared to the benefits of improving the basic incomes of a large number of workers.

Gary Huck--Huck/Konopacki Labor Cartoons. Used with permission

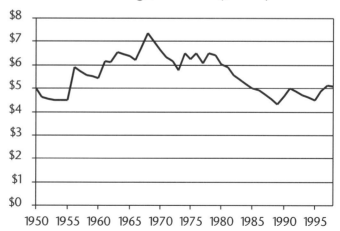

Minimum wage, 1950-98 **($1997)**

2.7 Shrinking Benefits

Workers do not live on take-home pay alone. In the 1960s, employers began providing relatively generous benefit packages, taking advantage of the fact that these were not subject to taxation. As these benefits became more and more expensive, however, employers began to change their minds.

In 1986, 95% of all large and medium-sized firms provided their employees with some medical insurance. By 1997, only 76% did so. A similar decline occurred in the number of businesses offering retirement benefits—from 89% in 1986 to 79% in 1997.

Getting time off to relax or recover from an illness is also becoming more difficult. Only 56% of large and medium firms gave their workers paid sick leave in 1997, down from 70% in 1986. The number offering paid holidays slipped from 99% to 89%.

Part-time and temporary workers, as well as those who work for small businesses, are even less likely to enjoy these benefits. In 1996, 64% of full-time workers in small firms received medical coverage and 46% got retirement benefits. Of part-time workers in small businesses, only 6% received health coverage and 13% retirement benefits.

Hmm... long hours for low pay, hands-on work with extremely toxic substances in a small unventilated room where rats nibble at my ankles and fellow bored co-workers stick me with pins for sport? But you say there's a health plan? I'll take it and I'll never leave.

© 1993 PETER HANNAN

Percent of workers in large and medium firms covered by medical care and retirement benefits

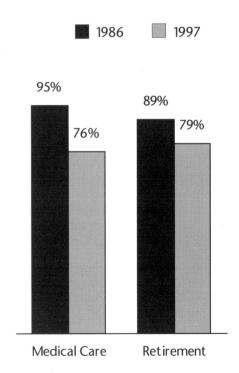

■ 1986   ▧ 1997

Medical Care: 95% (1986), 76% (1997)
Retirement: 89% (1986), 79% (1997)

2.8 Unequal Pay

Some workers have always gotten paid more than others, but differences in pay are becoming more extreme

The greatest inequalities exist among men. In 1997, the top 10% of male workers ranked by pay earned on average 4.5 times what the bottom 10% earned, up from 3.7 in 1979. An even larger increase in inequality over this period occurred among women. In 1979, the top 10% of women workers earned 2.7 times as much as the bottom 10%. By 1997, the top 10% were getting 4 times as much as the bottom 10%.

Several factors help explain this trend, including increases in imports made with cheap labor, the decline of union membership, and new technologies. However, public policies, such as the low minimum wage, also contribute.

r. jay magill

shhhh...

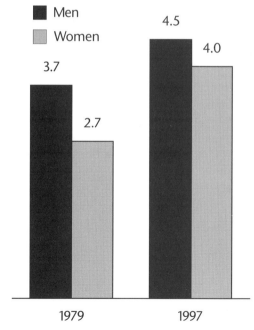

Ratio of wages of top 10 percent of employees to wages of bottom 10 percent

■ Men
▨ Women

1979: Men 3.7, Women 2.7
1997: Men 4.5, Women 4.0

2.9 The Working Poor

Many of the poor people in the United States are children or adults who are not in the labor force. However, a significant number of adults are classified as working poor—active in the labor market but falling below the poverty line.

- In 1996, the working poor numbered 7.4 million persons, or one out of every five poor people.

- Most of the working poor, 58 percent, had full-time jobs.

- Of all part-time workers, 12.4 percent fell below the poverty line, compared to 5.8 percent for the labor force as a whole.

- In 1997, about half, or 49.2 percent, of poor full-time workers had no health insurance.

Jim Morin

2.10 Living Wage Campaigns

From Baltimore to Los Angeles, cities across the country are using living wage ordinances to help lift low-paid workers out of poverty. The idea is simple: raise wages at the bottom to provide families with incomes they can live on. In most cases, only those firms doing business with the city are required to pay the living wage.

Opponents argue that higher wages mean fewer jobs. While the ordinances do increase labor costs, they often reach only a fraction of the municipal labor force. Studies predict that net employment effects will be small.

While living wage programs have changed the lives of a relatively small number of workers, the movement to bring a better standard of decency to low-income families has spread. As of August 1999, more than 40 cities and counties across the U.S. had adopted some form of living wage.

Major U.S. cities with living wage policies (as of May 1999)

Gary, IN (1991)	**New Haven, CT** (1997)
Baltimore, MD (1994)	**Oakland, CA** (1998)
Milwaukee, WI (1995)	**San Antonio, TX** (1998)
New York, NY (1996)	**Chicago, IL** (1998)
Portland, OR (1996)	**Detroit, MI** (1998)
Boston, MA (1997)	**San Jose, CA** (1998)
Minneapolis/St. Paul, MN (1997)	**Madison, WI** (1999)
Los Angeles, CA (1997)	**Miami-Dade County, FL** (1999)

r. jay magill

2.11 Underemployment

A job is a job is a job. Right? Not if it's part-time or temporary. Many workers in these positions would prefer full-time, permanent work.

To make matters more complicated, not everyone who wants a job but doesn't have one is counted as unemployed. Discouraged workers have stopped looking for work because of the sheer lack of opportunities where they live. Accounting for involuntary part-time workers and discouraged workers translates to an unemployment rate of 4.9% in 1997 into an underemployment rate of 8.9%.

Even full-time work can be precarious. The growth of jobs in the temporary help industry is shocking—from 417,000 jobs in 1982 to more than 2.5 million in 1997, an increase of over 530%.

Benefits are rare and pay is low in the temporary-help world. In 1997, temps received 65% of the average weekly earnings of someone in a non-temporary job; only 7% of these workers received any employer-provided health insurance.

Underemployed workers, by employment situation in 1998

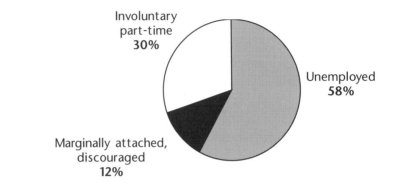

Involuntary part-time **30%**

Unemployed **58%**

Marginally attached, discouraged **12%**

Tom Tomorrow

2.12 Jobless in 1998

There's an old saying: if your neighbor can't find a job, the economy is suffering a recession. But if you're the one who can't find a job, it's a depression.

Some groups experience permanent depression. In 1998, the unemployment rate for whites reached a historically low 3.9%. African Americans were more than twice as likely to be unemployed, at a rate of 9.1%.

Teenagers are particularly vulnerable, with an unemployment rate of 14.6%. Even for those aged 20 to 24, the rate was far above average.

Being out of work is hard on people. Studies show that it contributes to problems like alcoholism, child abuse, and mental illness. Unemployment also means the economy is functioning below its potential. Putting more people to work can increase output and growth

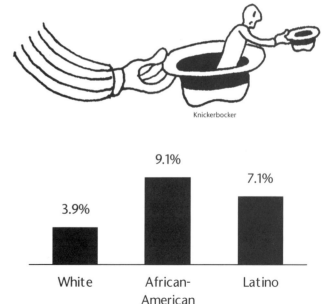

Knickerbocker

Unemployment rate in 1998, by age, race and Latino origin

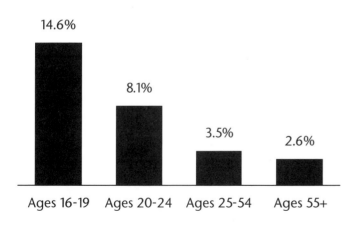

14.6%	8.1%	3.5%	2.6%
Ages 16-19	Ages 20-24	Ages 25-54	Ages 55+

3.9%	9.1%	7.1%
White	African-American	Latino

2.13 The Ups and Downs of Unemployment

Unemployment is like a roller coaster. When the economy grows, unemployment falls; when the economy slows down, unemployment zooms up.

Until around 1974, the annual unemployment rate was relatively low, between 3% and 6%. Then it began to increase, reaching a high of nearly 10% in the early 1980s and rarely falling below 6%. Recently the situation has improved. In 1997, the unemployment rate fell below 5% for the first time in nearly 25 years.

Less unemployment doesn't guarantee improved well-being, since more jobs don't always mean better jobs. Slow growth in earnings, more part-time and temporary work, and larger inequalities among workers have diminished the benefits.

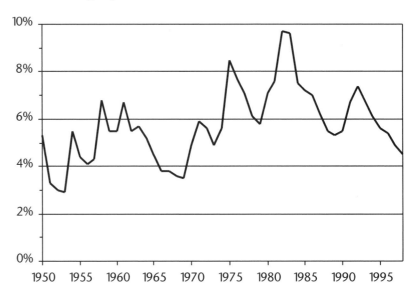

Unemployment rate, 1950-98

Russell Christian

44

2.14 Downsizing

Feeling a bit insecure? You should be. In 1996 the number of people affected by violent crimes was 2 million. The number affected by layoffs was 3 million. Polls show that about 20% of American adults were laid off permanently or had their jobs eliminated between 1981 and 1996. About 72% say that they or someone close to them has been affected by a layoff.

Most people who lose a job find another one. But only about 38% manage to find another full-time job at equal or higher pay. Many take a pay cut or lose benefits such as health insurance. Some are forced into the unemployment line or out of the labor force.

Some management consultants believe that rapid downsizing can do more hard than good.

A survey, released in 1997, of 62 major corporations reported that 70% were grappling with "serious problems of low morale and mistrust of management." But downsizing remains the quickest and easiest way for companies to cut their costs.

The consequences of being laid off from full-time permanent jobs (held at least 3 years), 1995-97

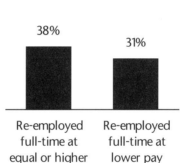

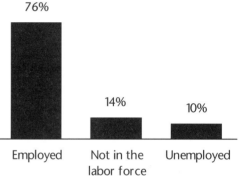

2.15 Who Belongs to Unions?

Ask someone to describe a typical union member and they'll probably imagine a white guy wearing a tool belt. The reality is very different. African Americans are more likely to be union members than white workers are, and Latinos have achieved a strong presence in the rank and file. Women are almost as likely as men to belong: 11% of women workers are unionized, compared to 16% of men.

Today union members find themselves in a wide variety of workplaces. Manufacturing jobs remain more heavily unionized than the services. With downsizing and the decline of factory jobs, the traditional base of unions has shrunk. Service jobs pose difficult challenges for organizers. However, many workers in the public sector, including teachers and police, are now unionized.

Percentage of all employees in various groups belonging to unions in 1998

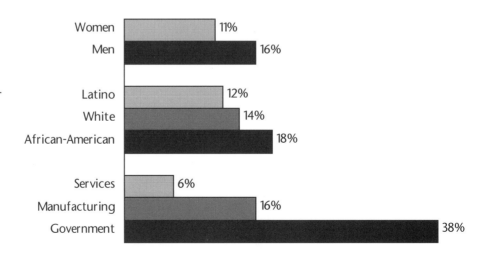

Women 11%
Men 16%

Latino 12%
White 14%
African-American 18%

Services 6%
Manufacturing 16%
Government 38%

2.16 The Comeback Kid

American unions have been through some rough times. Membership has fallen steadily, and many unions have been accused of failing to adapt to the changing nature of work in the U.S. In 1954, over 30% of workers belonged to unions. By 1997, this figure had plunged to about 15%.

However, unions are making a comeback. The ability to organize large-scale strikes has grown in recent years.

Unions have also begun to take up the challenges of organizing in the 90s. The successful 1997 strike of part-time UPS workers stands out as an example.

Many unions have historically discriminated against women and people of color. Today most recognize the strength of their diverse membership. Plus, they are actively involving a new generation of young people in their organizing efforts.

IT'S ALIVE!!

U.S. LABOR MOVEMENT

Gary Huck--Huck/Konopacki Labor Cartoons. Used with permission

Average number of workers per major strike or lockout

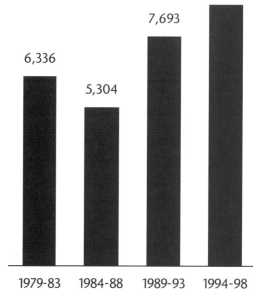

1979-83	1984-88	1989-93	1994-98
6,336	5,304	7,693	8,760

Chapter 3 **Women**

Russell Christian

You've come a long way—maybe. Imagine flipping on the television and watching a commercial about a tireless man who whisks the kids off to school after giving them an efficient but nutritious breakfast, and then starts on the day's laundry. You probably won't see it any time soon—a good reminder that both men and women have a long way to go to achieve a fair division of labor. A glance through this chapter will reveal that gender inequalities remain a central feature of our economic life.

How has women's place in the economy changed? As Chart 3.1 shows, most women now earn a wage. But their leisure time is much reduced because they continue to do most of the housework and child care. An increasing number also maintain families on their own. Chart 3.2 documents the decline in traditional married-couple families.

The good news is that women have narrowed the wage gap. Chart 3.3 points out substantial improvements in the relative earnings of full-time women wage-earners across all racial and ethnic groups. But equally qualified women should earn exactly what men earn. As Chart 3.4 indicates, they earn less than men do even in jobs that require substantial educational credentials, including computer programming and law.

Women have moved into many well-paying professional jobs once monopolized by men, as seen in Chart 3.5. But substantial barriers still prevent promotions to the top positions in major businesses. Chart 3.6 reveals some dimensions of the glass ceiling.

Women's traditional role in the household has always influenced their place in paid work. Chart 3.7 shows that many women workers remain in sex-typed and low-paid pink-collar jobs. Our economic system tends to undervalue caring labor. When performed in the home, such work is unpaid and often invisible. In the labor market, jobs in which people are primarily engaged in caring for dependents generally pay less than comparable work, as Chart 3.8 indicates.

Motherhood is economically risky for women. Chart 3.9 documents that over half of families living in poverty are maintained by women alone, a significant increase since 1959. Low levels of paternal child support increase the economic burden. Chart 3.10 shows that while unmarried mothers are now more likely to collect support, a basic pattern remains unchanged: Less than a third of all single mothers are receiving financial assistance from the fathers of their children.

The division of labor within the home remains unequal. Chart 3.11 points out that employed mothers in married-couple households spend much more time on child-care responsibilities than do employed fathers. Responsibilities on the job often conflict with those at home. Chart 3.12 documents the stress many women and men experience as both breadwinners and care providers.

With more women earning a wage, the demand for child care outside the home has grown. Chart 3.13 describes the different types of arrangements families make these days. International comparisons show that the U.S. government does less to support parenthood than do many other industrialized countries (Chart 3.14).

More young women are using contraceptives these days than ever before. Chart 3.15 shows that sexual behavior has changed in ways that help avert unintended pregnancies and limit the spread of sexually transmitted diseases. But in some ways, the scope for reproductive choice has actually narrowed as a result of attacks on abortion rights. Chart 3.16 describes some of these attacks, which include brutal acts of violence by so-called pro-life activists.

3.1 Most Women Earn a Wage

For more than a century, women's work has been shifting from the home to the factory, shop, and office. Since 1979, more than half of women over age 16 have been working or looking for work in the paid labor force.

Black women have historically been more likely than others to work for pay, largely because of the legacy of slavery, discrimination, and low family income. Today, however, there is little difference in the labor-force participation of women by race because white women have entered paid employment at a particularly rapid rate in recent years.

Mothers are the fastest-growing group within the labor force. By 1997, 64% of married women with children under age 6 were in the paid labor force, though a much smaller percentage (about 40%) worked 35 or more hours a week.

Many women who have joined the paid labor force find themselves working a double shift; they come home from their paid jobs and do additional unpaid work in the home—preparing meals, cleaning house, and looking after the kids.

Labor force participation rates for women, 1955-97

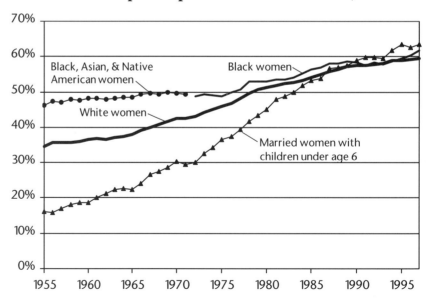

3.2 Married-Couple Families Are Less Common

Mom, Dad, Buddy and Sue aren't as likely to live together as they once were. They all want their own apartments. In 1960, 74% of all U.S. households were married-couple families. By 1997, only 53% of households fit this description. And less than half of these included children under 18.

More and more individuals, including the elderly, are choosing to live by themselves. Non-family households (mostly single persons) increased from 15% to 30% of the total between 1960 and 1997. The percentage of all households that are families maintained by women also increased, from 8% to 13%. Among families with children, women were particularly likely to be on their own. In 1997, about one of every four children under 18 was living with mom alone.

Getting married is still popular. But the amount of time that men and women stay married has gone down as the divorce rate has risen. Many blended families include children from a previous marriage, so step-moms and -dads play an increasingly important role.

The changing composition of households

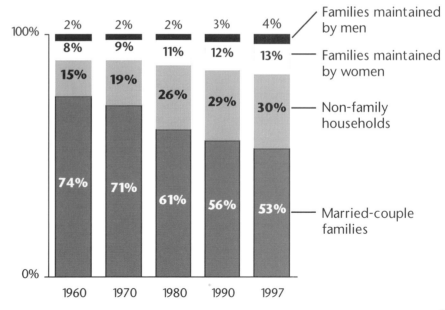

3.3 Women Still Earn Less Than Men

Women are gaining on men. Over the past 12 years, they have substantially improved their economic position. But in 1998, women working full-time still earned only about 76 cents for every dollar a man working full-time earned.

For a long time, women's relative earnings were stuck at about 60% of men's. Things began to change when they fought their way into advanced education and better-paying jobs.

Also, women were less affected than men were by the loss of well-paying manufacturing jobs in the 1980s. Because men's earnings increased hardly at all between 1979 and 1998, a modest increase in women's earnings had a big impact.

The difference between women's and men's wages is greatest among whites. Because African Americans and Latinos earn less overall, women in those groups earned more relative to men in 1998: 86% and 87% respectively, compared to 75% for whites.

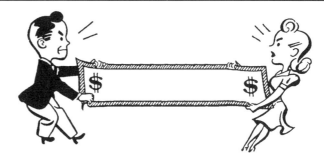

Women's earnings as a percentage of men's earnings (year-round, full-time workers)

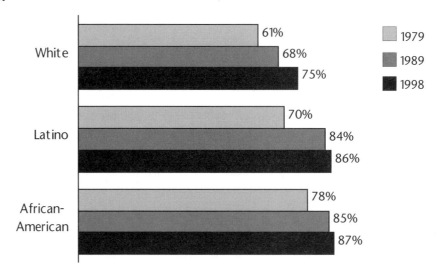

White
- 61% — 1979
- 68% — 1989
- 75% — 1998

Latino
- 70% — 1979
- 84% — 1989
- 86% — 1998

African-American
- 78% — 1979
- 85% — 1989
- 87% — 1998

3.4 Equal Work, Unequal Pay

More than 20 years ago, the Equal Pay Act made it illegal to pay women less for doing the same work as men. Of course, in most cases, they don't do the same work, so the law is difficult to enforce. That's why most of women's gains have come from entering new, traditionally male occupations.

Even within the same occupation, however, pay differentials are glaring: female computer programmers and lawyers earn significantly less than males in those jobs. Some, but not all, of this disparity is explained by differences in age and in experience on the job. Within occupations, women are often segregated in the specialties that pay the least.

Many women don't know and aren't allowed to ask how much they earn relative to men in their workplace. It is risky and expensive to sue an employer, and the Equal Employment Opportunity Commission can help only a small number of people.

Several recent lawsuits have vindicated women who were willing to fight for their rights. In January 1999, Texaco Inc. agreed to pay $3.1 million to 186 women who were, according to the Department of Labor, systematically underpaid relative to their male counterparts. In 1998, Merrill Lynch agreed to the settlement of a gender discrimination suit, allowing any of the 2,500 women who have worked as brokers since 1994 to bring claims for compensation.

Tom Tomorrow

Women's median wages as a percentage of men's median wages in 1997

Computer programmers	85%
Lawyers	76%
Managers of marketing, advertising, public relations	69%
Machine operators, assemblers, inspectors	70%

53

3.5 Nice Work if You Can Get It

More women are climbing the professional job ladder. In the 1950s and 1960s, they were often blocked from entering fields such as engineering and medicine. But in the 1970s, a militant women's movement helped open the door. Affirmative-action programs were particularly effective at improving women's opportunities to pursue advanced educational degrees.

By 1997, women accounted for 9% of all engineers, 28% of all lawyers and judges, 45% of all managers, and 23% of all doctors. While this trend strengthened the women's movement by putting more women into positions of power, it also intensified the divisive impact of class and race differences among women.

Nice work if you can get it, but it helps to come from a family that can help pay the bills for college and graduate school.

Women in professions
(as a percentage of total in those professions)

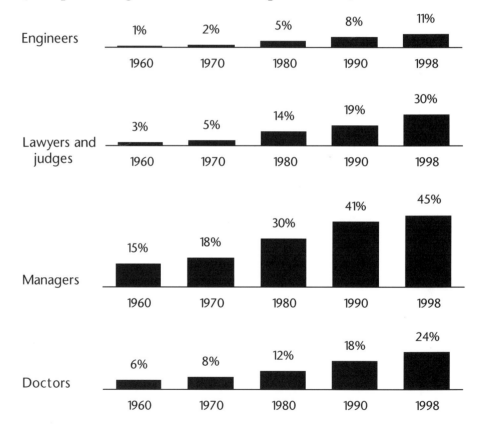

3.6 Glass Ceilings

It may be hard to see, but it hurts when you bump your head against it. A glass ceiling is a barrier to upward mobility largely based on hidden bias and unspoken assumptions. In spite of growing diversity in the workforce, women and minorities are seriously underrepresented in management positions.

An annual census of the Fortune 500 corporations by Catalyst, the consulting firm, found that only 11% of corporate officers—and 3% of the highest-paid officers—were women. The definition of "officer" was taken from the companies' own public filings.

Some companies do better than others. At Nordstrom, Fannie Mae, and Pacificare, women hold down 40% of officers' slots. But at General Electric, Compaq, Philip Morris, Intel, and Exxon, no women are found in the upper echelons.

Women as a percentage of all officers in Fortune 500 companies in 1998

©1999 magill, jr.

3.7 Pink-Collar Jobs

Women have specialized in jobs that don't fit the traditional blue-collar/white-collar distinction. They represent the overwhelming majority of workers in jobs such as nursing, teaching, secretarial, and personal service. Within more detailed occupational categories, segregation is often even more extreme.

Such occupational segregation puts women at an economic disadvantage. The greater the number of women relative to men in an occupation, the lower the average pay. Why don't more women choose to enter traditional male jobs? They may face discrimination from employers or harassment from fellow workers. They may like working with other women doing tasks that involve helping others. They may also worry that "unfeminine" choices will lower their chances of success in dating and marriage.

Whatever their reasons for entering pink-collar jobs, most women would like to see more room for career advancement and better pay.

Women as a percentage of all employees in selected occupations in 1997

Registered Nurses	92%
Teachers, except college and university	74%
Secretaries, stenographers, typists	98%
Personal-service occupations	73%

Nicole Hollander

56

3.8 The Care Penalty

The labor market does not reward care for other people. Jobs involving face-to-face interaction with young children are very poorly paid compared to jobs that require far less skill and responsibility. Parking lot attendants and bus drivers, for instance, earn substantially more than child-care workers and preschool teachers.

Pay-equity policies could address this problem. In Australia, such policies have helped increase women's earnings to about 91% of men's.

It's not just women who are affected by the care penalty. Child-care workers are better-educated than the general population and often capable of getting higher earnings and more benefits in other jobs. As a result, their turnover rates are high—about one-third of child-care workers leave their jobs every year. The overall quality of care that children receive probably suffers as a result.

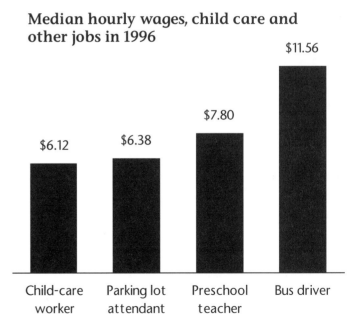

Median hourly wages, child care and other jobs in 1996

Child-care worker	Parking lot attendant	Preschool teacher	Bus driver
$6.12	$6.38	$7.80	$11.56

3.9 Mothers, Children, and Poverty

Mothers on their own have always been particularly vulnerable to poverty, but over the past 25 years their situation has worsened. Their families represented 55% of all those below the poverty line in 1997, compared to 48% in 1976.

This feminization of poverty reflects, in part, the pauperization of motherhood. Support from both fathers and the state has diminished in recent years, increasing the economic burden on mothers. Raising the next generation of workers and taxpayers is apparently not considered productive work.

Changes in welfare implemented in 1996 have helped move many mothers off public assistance. But few of the jobs they have moved into offer wages sufficient to keep themselves and their children out of poverty. Child support enforcement remains a serious problem.

It's not just single mothers who suffer. The threat of poverty reduces married women's bargaining power in the home.

Percentage of all poor families maintained by women alone

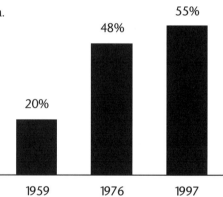

1959	1976	1997
20%	48%	55%

DID YOU KNOW THAT THE AVERAGE WOMAN'S STANDARD OF LIVING DROPS 73% DURING THE FIRST YEAR AFTER A DIVORCE?

DID YOU KNOW THAT THE AVERAGE MAN'S STANDARD OF LIVING IMPROVES 42% DURING THAT SAME YEAR?

I WILL ALWAYS LOVE YOU.

Ted Rall

3.10 Deadbeat Dads

Sometimes you see their faces on "Wanted" posters, or hear about their wages being garnished. But most deadbeat dads are still on the loose. Less than a third of single mothers today receive child support from the fathers of their children, a figure that has remained largely the same since 1976, despite major changes in enforcement laws.

The overall trend does conceal improvements for never-married mothers and their children—18% now receive child support, compared to only 5% in 1976. It is easier to establish biological parenthood now than it once was. In addition, many states threaten to deny public assistance to unmarried mothers who fail to reveal paternity and aggressively pursue delinquent fathers, requiring them to help reimburse taxpayers for welfare costs.

Divorced and separated women tend to be more affluent. Their overall probability of getting child support is higher (about 42%), but has increased only slightly over time. Enforcement problems have generated a brand-new industry—private detectives who track down delinquent spouses in return for a share of the settlement.

A single mother is more likely to be never-married today than twenty years ago. This change has countervailed improvements within the never-married category, leaving the overall percentage of single mothers getting child support virtually unchanged.

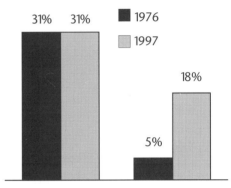

Percent of single mothers receiving child support, by marital status, 1976 and 1997

- ■ 1976
- ▨ 1997

All single mothers: 31% (1976), 31% (1997)
Never-married single mothers: 5% (1976), 18% (1997)

Ted Rall

3.11 Working Parents

Dads who live with their children seem to be changing more diapers than they used to. Still, employed mothers spend a lot more time than fathers caring for or doing things with children. And when time for all tasks is added up, employed mothers spend about an hour more each workday on home chores.

Child care is shared more evenly among working parents doing shift work with, for instance, one person working nights. Of course, that means that couples don't have much overlapping time at home to spend with each other.

The U.S. doesn't collect nearly as much information about time use as it does about other things like consumer expenditures or earnings. But one thing is clear: Parents often feel stressed. In 1998, 65% of parents surveyed said they would reduce their paid hours of work if they could.

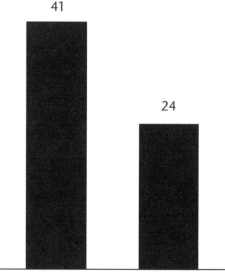

Hours per week caring for or doing things with children, married couples in 1997

41

24

Employed Mothers   Employed Fathers

3.12 Work/Family Conflicts

- **Only 50% of employed parents** in the U.S. are able to take a few days off from work to care for sick children without losing pay, forfeiting vacation time, or having to make up some excuse for leaving work.

- **Asked in 1997 how often** they felt they lacked enough time for their family or other important people in their life because of their jobs, 33% of employees with children under 18 answered "Often or very often."

- **Elder care, as well as child care**, is a big responsibility. About 25% of all workers provided special assistance to someone 65 years or older in 1996.

- **Changes in health care practices**, including shorter hospital stays, increase the burden of informal care. About 20% of adults provide some sort of daily care for a person with a chronic health problem.

- **Women are particularly likely** to take on caregiving responsibilities. They often make large economic sacrifices and experience physical and mental stress.

Barrie Maguire

3.13 The Demand for Child Care

others in our society are now expected to work for pay. They are not eligible for public assistance unless they do. But good child care is hard to find and expensive to pay for. In dual-earner families, spouses help one another out. Even among this group, however, child-care centers and other forms of non-relative care are indispensable.

Half of American parents with young children earn less than $35,000 per year. Yet unsubsidized child-care costs between $4,000 and $10,000 per year for a single child. Many low-income working families cannot find subsidized care.

New York state, for instance, provides subsidies to only one in ten eligible children.

Some states, like Georgia and California, are moving towards public provision of preschool education of four- and five-year olds.

Child care arrangements for youngest child not in school in 1997, dual-earner families

child-care subsidy,
no child-care subsidy,
no child-care subsidy,
child-care subsidy...

r. jay magill

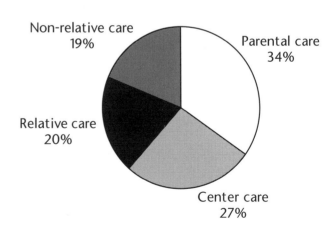

Non-relative care
19%

Parental care
34%

Relative care
20%

Center care
27%

3.14 Family Policies in Europe

The parental leave and child-care benefits given to working families in the United States are the least generous in the industrialized world.

- About 80% of industrialized countries offer paid maternity leave to women workers. Canada gives 17 weeks. In the U.S., all we have is the Family and Medical Leave Act of 1993, which permits up to 12 weeks of unpaid leave.

- In Sweden, parental leaves can be shared or used by one parent, but one non-transferable month is reserved for the father and one for the mother, to encourage sharing. During their child's first year, more than one-half of fathers use some leave. Fathers use nearly one-third of all paid temporary leave to stay home and care for sick children under twelve.

- Family allowances (regular payments to help support children) are offered by most countries of Western Europe. The U.S. allows parents to deduct money from their taxable income for children as dependents. But the value of this deduction as a percentage of family income has declined over time. Tripling the current deduction would restore the relative value it had in 1948.

Nicole Hollander

3.15 Safe Sex

Planned Parenthood puts it this way: "It is normal to want to enhance love and intimacy by having sex. And it is normal to want to have sex without causing pregnancy and without getting a sexually transmitted infection."

Teenage pregnancy has dropped over the last twenty years, both because fewer teens are having sex and more are using contraception. The percentage of teen women using some form of contraception increased from 48% in 1982 to 78% in 1995. Many are using condoms, and injectable contraceptives have increased in popularity.

Evidence shows that publicly funded contraceptive services avert many unintended pregnancies every year. But many young people still lack information and access. Teen pregnancy rates in the U.S. remain twice as high as in England and in Canada.

Sex education could also help prevent the spread of the HIV virus that causes AIDS.

A 1993 study of couples in which one partner had HIV showed that using condoms during every act of intercourse prevented HIV transmission for all but two of 171 women. Eight out of ten women whose partners did not use condoms became infected.

Cyann Brolfe

Contraceptive use at first intercourse for women age 15 to 19

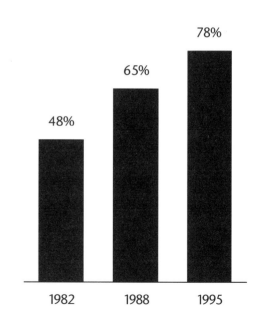

3.16 Reproductive Rights and Wrongs

The 1990s have not been good for reproductive rights. Roe vs. Wade, a Supreme Court decision made in 1973, promised women the right to a safe and legal abortion. Many poor, young, and rural women find this promise an empty one.

- Abortions are not uncommon among those who can afford them. In 1996 they numbered about 26% of all pregnancies, not counting miscarriages.

- Since 1976, the Hyde amendment has banned federal funding for all abortions (except in cases of rape, incest, or threat to the mother's life). Mothers on public assistance cannot obtain abortions through Medicaid.

- Teens who give birth are more likely to come from poor or low-income families (83%) than are teens who undergo abortions (61%). In 1996, 86% of all U.S. counties had no identified abortion provider. Many states have passed laws imposing restrictions on abortion access, such as mandatory delays and biased information laws.

- Since 1993, three doctors, three clinic employees, and a clinic escort have been murdered by anti-abortion activists. There have been more than a dozen attempted murders, and arson and bombings at clinics have become common.

Russell Christian

65

Chapter 4 **People of Color**

Russell Christian

important source of diversity; Chart 4.3 outlines the shifting movements of people to this country. While the number of immigrants relative to our population is higher than it was in the 1950s, it remains far lower than it was in the first decade of this century.

Most metropolitan areas remain highly segregated by race. Chart 4.4 summarizes the geographical differences that lead to the concentration of poverty. People of color in poor neighborhoods are particularly likely to experience joblessness. As Chart 4.5 indicates, the unemployment rate for African Americans and Latinos has always been substantially higher than the rate for whites. Even with the recent drop in unemployment, rates for people of color are nearly twice those for whites.

Chart 4.6 shows that differences in educational attainment can't fully explain these differences. In 1998, Latino college graduates were more likely to be unemployed than were white high school graduates. Still, educational attainment does matter, and a far smaller proportion of African Americans and Latinos than of whites are college graduates, as Chart 4.7 demonstrates.

People of color are more likely than whites to end up in dead-end jobs. Chart 4.8 shows that they are overrepresented in less-skilled service occupations and underrepresented in managerial and professional positions. The result is obvious: inequalities in earnings.

Economic opportunities in America are determined both by the color of people's skin and by the contents of their wallets. While it's hard to find data describing the fate of every ethnic group, statistics show that African Americans and Latinos are more likely than whites to die in infancy, to grow up in poverty, to experience unemployment, and to spend time in prison.

Chart 4.1 describes the composition of the U.S. population in 1998, while Chart 4.2 explores the ethnic diversity of Latinos, Asians, and Pacific Islanders in more detail. Immigration has always provided an

Chart 4.9 compares the weekly earnings of men and women of color relative to those of whites. In recent years, these inequalities have gotten worse.

High unemployment, unequal educational opportunities, and low-paying jobs have a cumulative effect. As Chart 4.10 illustrates, Latinos and African Americans are more susceptible to poverty than whites are.

Unemployment figures for people of color would look much worse if the prison population were included in the statistics. Incarceration rates in the United States are much higher than in other developed countries, and as Chart 4.11 shows, a much higher percentage of African-American than white men are in prison. Disruptive effects on family life are reflected in reduced opportunities for black women to marry partners of their own race, documented in Chart 4.12.

Single-mother households face enormous economic challenges and a high risk of poverty. Chart 4.13 demonstrates that African-American and Latino households are more likely to be maintained by women alone. Plus, as Chart 4.14 indicates, a larger fraction of families of color are raising children, performing the largely unpaid work of rearing the next generation of workers and taxpayers.

Discrimination remains a problem. Chart 4.15 shows that people of color face a much higher denial rate for small business loans. Chart 4.16 documents recent efforts to roll back affirmative action.

4.1 Who We Are

The U.S. has traditionally been described as a melting pot, but a better metaphor would be a salad bowl. In 1998, more than a quarter of the population had ethnic backgrounds that set them apart from the culturally and politically dominant white population.

African Americans and Latinos accounted for 12% and 11% of the population, respectively. Asians made up about 4% and Native Americans about 1%. Because these groups are concentrated in certain geographic areas, they often represent a much larger percentage of the population in their own communities.

All these groups are growing faster than the white population. Ethnic diversity is here to stay.

Cyann Brolfe

Racial and ethnic composition of the U.S. population (projections)

	1998	**2050**
White	73%	53%
African-American	12%	14%
Latino	11%	25%
Asian	4%	8%
Native American	1%	1%

4.2 Asian and Latino Diversity

Many people strongly identify with their families' nation of origin. The broad ethnic categories used by the Census Bureau conceal enormous diversity, particularly among Latinos, Asians, and Pacific Islanders.

Individuals with a Mexican heritage represented 60% of the Latino population in 1990, concentrated largely in the Southwest, where many have lived for generations. Puerto Ricans were the second-largest category, followed by Cubans and by those from other countries of Central or South America, many of whom are recent immigrants.

Among Asians or Pacific Islanders, Chinese and Filipinos are the most numerous. Most Japanese and Chinese have long been citizens, and Hawaiians are native to this country. Other groups include many recent immigrants.

Latinos, Asians, and Pacific Islanders will become a much stronger presence in the 21st century. In 1995, there were seven white people for every Latino and 21 whites for every Asian or Pacific Islander. By 2050, Census Bureau estimates put these ratios at 2:1 and 6:1, respectively.

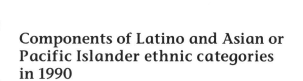

Knickerbocker

Components of Latino and Asian or Pacific Islander ethnic categories in 1990

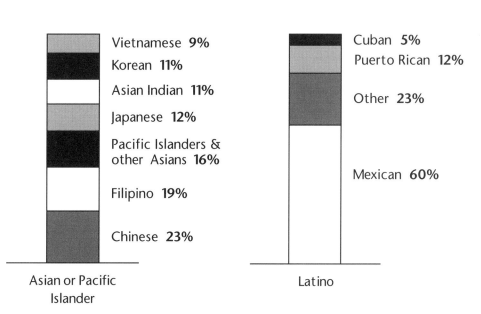

Vietnamese **9%**

Korean **11%**

Asian Indian **11%**

Japanese **12%**

Pacific Islanders & other Asians **16%**

Filipino **19%**

Chinese **23%**

Asian or Pacific Islander

Cuban **5%**

Puerto Rican **12%**

Other **23%**

Mexican **60%**

Latino

4.3 New Citizens

The Statue of Liberty has welcomed many waves of immigration to this country. The number of new entrants relative to the existing population was higher in the first half of the 1990s than in the 1950s. But by historical standards the official immigration rate remained quite low. In the first decade of the twentieth century, about one immigrant entered per year for every 100 members of the U.S. population. Between 1991 and 1995, the rate was less than half that, at .4 per 100.

Studies show that legal immigrants are not a drain on our economy. Today, they are more likely to have college degrees than our own citizens are. Those who entered this country before 1980 now have an average household income higher than that of native-born Americans, and they contribute more in taxes. Undocumented workers are not officially eligible for benefits, and even legal immigrants are effectively prohibited from receiving most forms of public assistance.

The immigrants who are most economically disadvantaged are political refugees from countries such as Vietnam and the former Soviet Union.

Mike Konpocki, Huck/Konopacki Labor Cartoons. Used with permission.

Average annual number of immigrants per 100 U.S. population

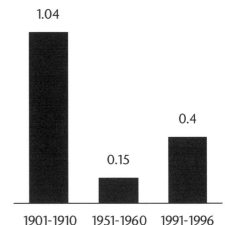

4.4 Neighborhoods in Black and White

- **Between 1970 and 1990,** black-white segregation levels declined dramatically in heavily white cities such as Albuquerque, Tucson, and Phoenix .

- **But in metropolitan areas** with high concentrations of African Americans, such as New York and Chicago, extreme segregation is the norm, and has diminished only slightly since 1970.

- **Intense segregation** results in a concentration of poverty 27% greater than it would be under complete integration.

- **Three-quarters of African Americans,** but only about 10% of whites, Latinos, and Asians, are highly segregated.

- **Harvard researchers found** that the percentage of minority students enrolled in schools with a substantial white enrollment fell between 1991 and 1994 as Federal courts made it easier for school districts to abandon desegregation plans.

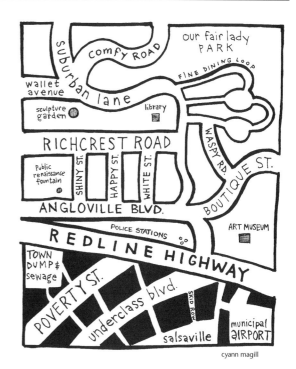

cyann magill

4.5 Last Hired

Unemployment is a game of musical chairs. When the music stops, not everyone has a seat, and it is mostly African Americans and Latinos who are left standing. In 1998, 8% of black workers and 7% of Latinos could not find jobs, while only 4% of whites were in the same predicament.

Teenagers had an even harder time. The unemployment rate among black youths ages 16-19 was 30%; among whites it was 14%. Persistently high unemployment rates discourage people from looking for work. Black male labor force participation rates have dropped considerably in recent years.

Black workers are often the first fired as well as the last hired; they suffered disproportionately from job cuts during the 1990-91 recession. By bearing a large share of the burden of unemployment, people of color buffer whites against the ups and downs of the business cycle.

Unemployment rate by race and Latino origin, 1973-98 (civilian workers age 16 and above)

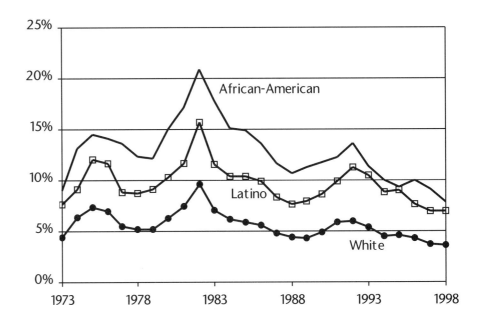

4.6 Unemployment by Degrees

A college diploma confers real advantages, including lower unemployment, higher wages, and better health. Unemployment rates are highest among those lacking a high school diploma. But racial/ethnic differences remain significant even when education is taken into account. College-educated African Americans and Latinos had higher unemployment rates than their white counterparts in 1998.

Perhaps some of them were considered "overqualified" for the jobs they applied for. If affirmative action was really leading to reverse discrimination, as some critics argue, one would expect to see exactly the opposite pattern. It seems that educated whites have an easier time finding jobs than do members of any other ethnic group.

Latinos without high school diplomas have lower rates of unemployment than African Americans in the same category. This probably reflects regional differences. There is greater demand for agricultural and outdoor workers in the West, where many Latinos are concentrated.

Youth unemployment, by educational attainment in 1998 (individuals age 16-24)

	Diploma		
	None	High school	College
White	15.5%	5.8%	3.0%
African-American	34.1%	13.1%	3.4%
Latino	14.1%	8.4%	6.3%

Jacob Lawrence

4.7 The Education Gap Persists

Access to college is improving more rapidly for whites than for other groups. Racial and ethnic differences in education have always been greatest on the college level, and they have intensified over time.

Both African Americans and Latinos have made significant progress in getting high school diplomas. In 1997, almost 75% of African Americans over age 25, and 55% of Latinos, had completed 4 or more years of high school. But less than 14% of either group had completed 4 or more years of college.

Cuts in aid for college students reinforced a decline in the percentage of low-income high school graduates going on to college. Budget cuts also shrank tutorial and counseling programs for disadvantaged students. The long-run economic consequences are ominous. In 1997, high school graduates earned only a little more than half of what college graduates earned.

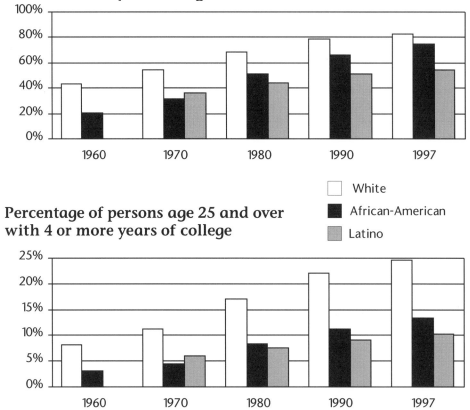

Percentage of persons age 25 and over with 4 or more years of high school

Percentage of persons age 25 and over with 4 or more years of college

White
African-American
Latino

4.8 More Menial Work

Historically, people of color have been confined to jobs whites wanted to avoid, like domestic service. Today, they work mostly in jobs that involve housekeeping for the economy as a whole, such as sweeping halls, preparing food, waiting on tables, and caring for children.

About a fifth of African Americans and Latinos work at the low end of the occupational ladder, in poorly paid service jobs. Not surprisingly, they are underrepresented in managerial and professional occupations. Only 21% of African Americans and 15% of Latinos held such jobs in 1998, compared with 31% of all white workers.

Despite the visibility of a few highly-paid basketball players and media stars, few families of color enjoy an affluent lifestyle. Only 4% of African-American households and 7% of Latino households had incomes over $100,000 in 1997, compared with 13% of white households.

Knickerbocker

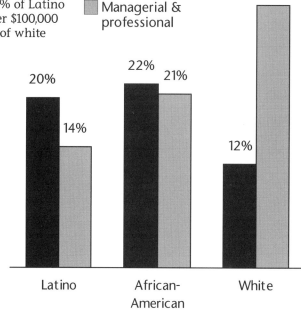

Employed civilians, by occupation, race, and Latino origin in 1997

- ■ Service
- ▨ Managerial & professional

Latino: 20% (Service), 14% (Managerial & professional)
African-American: 22% (Service), 21% (Managerial & professional)
White: 12% (Service), 31% (Managerial & professional)

75

4.9 Wage Inequalities

For a while, it seemed like the playing field was leveling out. In the 1960s and early 1970s, African-American, Native American, and Asian workers (labeled "non-white" by the Census Bureau at that time) narrowed the gap between their earnings and those of white workers.

A long-standing trend has been reversed. Between 1979 and 1998, most men and women of color lost ground relative to whites of the same gender. While the median weekly earnings of African-American men as a percentage of those of white men remained unchanged at 76%, the relative earnings of African-American women and Latino men and women declined.

Increased racial inequality reflects the growing pay gap between less educated and more educated workers. Cutbacks in government jobs and a weakened commitment to fighting racial discrimination have also played parts.

Median weekly earnings of African Americans and Latinos as a percentage of those of whites (full-time workers)

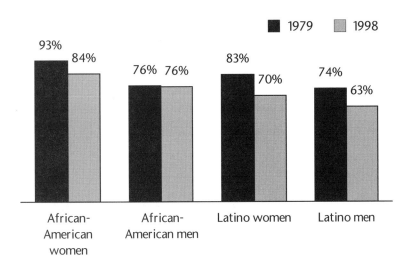

■ 1979　▨ 1998

- African-American women: 93%, 84%
- African-American men: 76%, 76%
- Latino women: 83%, 70%
- Latino men: 74%, 63%

Mike Konopacki—Huck/Konopacki Labor Cartoons. Used with permission

4.10 The Color of Poverty

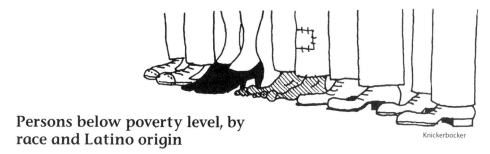

Knickerbocker

Many people think poverty is somebody else's problem, and racism makes it easier to blame the victim. But history shows that poverty is systemic. Inherited inequalities, discrimination, unemployment, and rips in the social safety net have left African Americans and Latinos more susceptible to poverty than whites are.

Between 1959 and 1978, government antipoverty programs and relatively low unemployment rates decreased the overall poverty rate and reduced the differences in poverty rates among ethnic groups. Things got worse in the 1980s and early 1990s. Unemployment went up, and cuts in federal social spending had a particularly ugly impact on people of color. Public support for families with dependent children declined, leaving many kids vulnerable to squalor and violence.

Poverty rates fell with the economic expansion of the late 1990s. But even in 1997, a year of exceptionally low unemployment rates, more than a quarter of all African Americans and Latinos lived in families with incomes below the poverty line.

Persons below poverty level, by race and Latino origin

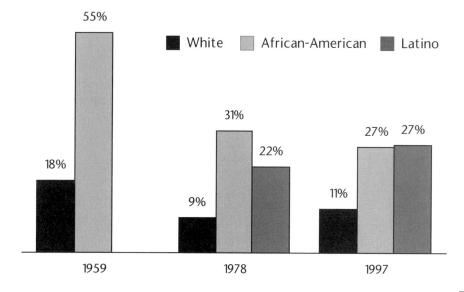

■ White　■ African-American　■ Latino

1959: 18%, 55%
1978: 9%, 31%, 22%
1997: 11%, 27%, 27%

4.11 Doing Time

Incarceration rates in the United States are higher than in any other political democracy in the world, and prisoners are disproportionately black. The 711,600 African-American men in jails and prisons in 1995 represented almost 7% of the total black male population.

One out of twenty Americans born this year is likely to spend some time in a correctional facility. For African Americans, the odds are far higher—one out of four.

A majority of inmates—nearly 60% in the Federal system—are drug offenders. Americans don't use more drugs than people in other countries do. But if they are caught, they are far more likely to go to jail. Mandatory sentencing rules leave judges with little discretion, even for individuals arrested for simple possession of a small quantity of an illicit drug.

The social costs of incarceration are very high. For one thing, it costs more to keep a man in prison than to send him to college. Jail time doesn't exactly help develop social or labor force skills, and it has a disruptive effect on families.

r. jay magill

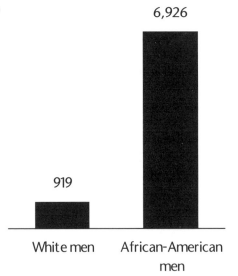

Number of adults held in state or federal prisons or local jails, per 100,000 adult residents, in 1995

4.12 Marriageable Men

Black women are far less likely to marry than white women are, even if they become mothers. One reason is that most marriages take place among individuals of the same race, and the cumulative effect of poverty, unemployment, and incarceration takes a lot of black men out of circulation.

Defining a "marriageable person" as someone one who is 18 or older, and neither in prison nor, if male, unemployed, there were only 73 marriageable black men for every 100 marriageable black women in 1995. The odds were far better for white women.

Another factor makes these odds even worse—black men are far more likely to marry white women than white men are to marry black women.

Demographic differences like these have cultural consequences. Black women have become more self-reliant, and nearly one in four young, single black men say that they never want to marry.

r. jay magill

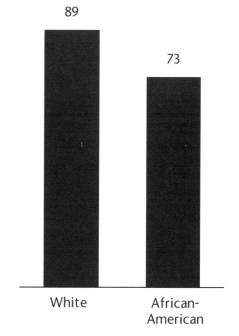

Number of marriageable men per 100 marriageable women in 1995

89 — White

73 — African-American

4.13 Women Maintaining Families

Mothers on their own are forced to cope with the triple burden of paying the bills, doing the housework, and looking after the kids. The proportion of families maintained by women alone has increased among all ethnic groups, but is especially high among people of color. In 1997, 47% of African-American families and 24% of all Latino families fell into this category.

These families are highly susceptible to poverty, because they typically rely on the earnings of a single adult and incur expenses for child care. Because child support enforcement is poor, few receive substantial transfers from absent parents. Because levels of public assistance are low, many live in poverty even if they are "on welfare."

Some policymakers argue that public assistance programs have promoted female headship. But such programs have varied considerably across states, and the percentage of families maintained by women alone has never been significantly lower in states with low benefits. Female headship has increased significantly among affluent as well as poor families.

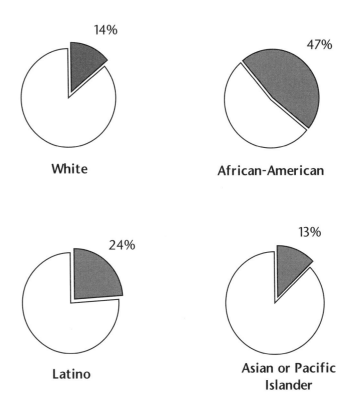

Families maintained by women alone in 1997

14% — White

47% — African-American

24% — Latino

13% — Asian or Pacific Islander

4.14 Who's Raising the Kids?

African-American and Latino families have more kids than white families do. In 1998, fewer than half of all married-couple white families had any children under age 18, compared with 51% of African-American and 66% of Latino families. The differences are even greater if all families, rather than just married-couple families, are taken into account.

All citizens depend on a future generation of workers to pay off public debt and provide support for the older generation through Social Security taxes. But public support for child rearing remains quite slim, and parenthood often leads to poverty.

The fact that many children are children of color may be one of the reasons why political priorities have shifted away from programs that benefit children, such as welfare, public education, and job training.

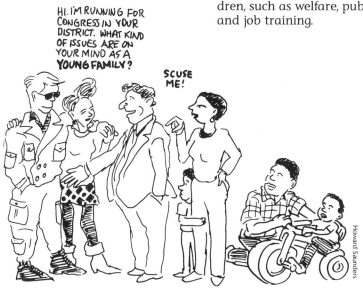

Families with children under 18 as a percentage of all married-couple families, by race and Latino origin, in 1997

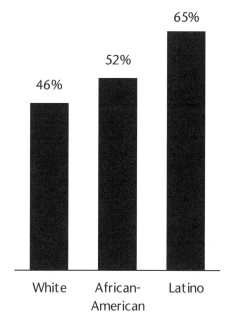

White	African-American	Latino
46%	52%	65%

81

4.15 Lending Discrimination

Knickerbocker

"**M**ost of those people don't want to borrow money—and those who do have a terrible credit history." That's the explanation bankers initially gave when systematic differences in lending to whites, Latinos, and African Americans were revealed. But in 1992, the Federal Reserve Bank of Boston performed a detailed statistical analysis of mortgage applications, and found evidence of discrimination. Another study shows that black home-owners tend to pay higher interest rates.

Small businesses are affected as well. An analysis of the National Survey of Small Business Finances of 1993 showed that blacks were about twice as likely to be denied credit, even after controlling for differences in credit-worthiness and other factors. It seems that few loan applicants have a flawless credit history, and most need some advice and the benefit of the doubt in order to get their loan. Predominantly white loan officers are most likely to extend such generosity to people who look and act like them.

Denial rate for small business loans in 1993

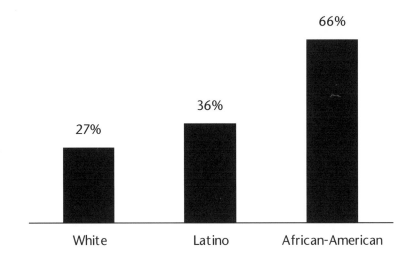

4.16 Affirmative Action

Most voters support the principles of diversity and a level playing field. Affirmative action is under attack, but it is being staunchly defended by advocates of equal opportunity. Bills to outlaw it have been defeated in over ten state legislatures, as well as in Congress.

Affirmative action remains in effect at most elite colleges, and a major study concludes these policies "created the backbone of the black middle class." Without affirmative action, black and Latino enrollments will probably suffer.

Suspension of affirmative action procedures at the University of California at Berkeley resulted in a 57% drop in blacks enrolled, and a 40% drop in Latinos. Eight hundred black applicants with a 4.0 grade average and scores of at least 1,200 on the Scholastic Aptitude exam were turned away.

At the University of Texas, a new rule requiring admission of the top 10% of students from every high school in the state has significantly increased undergraduate enrollments of blacks and Latinos, but has had little effect on access to law and medical school.

Matt Wuerker

Chapter 5 **Government**

Russell Christian

Some people denounce Big Government as the source of all our economic woes. Others worry about priorities, lamenting a government that spends neither wisely nor well. Still others point to gaping holes in service provision and the need for more public expenditures in vital areas.

This chapter takes a critical look at the U.S. government, with a focus on spending and taxation. By breaking down expenditures into federal, state and local, and private sector components, Chart 5.1 tries to answer this question: How big is government, anyway? Chart 5.2 offers an international comparison. Relative to other in-

dustrialized countries, our public sector is relatively small as a percentage of Gross Domestic Product (GDP).

Chart 5.3 looks at the composition of federal spending and how it has changed over time. While military spending has fallen as a fraction of the total from 1968 to 1998, interest payments have more than doubled. During the same period, Social Security and Medicare programs claimed a larger share of Federal dollars. Chart 5.4 looks more closely at trends in social spending, documenting cuts in the share of education, training, community development, and social assistance programs.

The military budget continues to consume a large portion of federal funds. While the military has claimed a smaller share since the end of the Cold War, total expenditures remain high. As Chart 5.5 points out, the cost of high-tech weaponry seems particularly extreme when compared to the educational and child-care services this money could buy. Chart 5.6 shows how our military budget towers over those of other countries around the world.

After years of running a budget deficit, the federal government suddenly finds itself with a surplus of funds. Chart 5.7 traces the movement from surplus to deficit and back again from the 1950s to the present. A surplus of funds doesn't mean that the burden of government debt has vanished, as Chart 5.8 shows. In the 1980s, the Federal government racked up sizeable debts through policies of lower taxation and high military spending. These debts still must be paid.

What about the tax side? Chart 5.9 documents where Federal revenues come from. Today corporations are paying a smaller share of taxes, while individuals are paying more. The current system takes a bigger bite out of low and middling earnings than out of higher ones. Chart 5.10 describes how the tax burden accounts for a larger share of the earnings of low-income than rich families. Chart 5.11 tracks the decline in corporate taxes over the years.

Lower taxes aren't the only benefits corporations get from government. Chart 5.12 shows how industrial contributions influence the development of laws and regulations. Lobbying has become big business. Chart 5.13 suggests that the deafening roar of moneyed interests may discourage ordinary people from trying to make their voices heard. Voter participation has dropped steadily since the 1960s. Not surprisingly, efforts to end welfare "as we know it" hurt the poor more than the affluent. Chart 5.14 describes some of the most notorious giveaways.

With the average age of the American population rising, many people are worrying about the future of Social Security. Chart 5.15 looks at spending over time and examines the pressures for change. Adjustments to the system will probably be needed in the future, but a major overhaul appears unnecessary. Chart 5.16 explains why privatizing Social Security is a bad idea.

5.1 How Big is Government?

Many people complain about "Big Government." But how big is big? In 1998, direct federal outlays amounted to $1,423 billion; state and local governments spent about $989 billion. Compare these totals to the gross domestic product (GDP) of $8,511 billion.

Taxpayers get a lot back for what they put in. Public schools educate most Americans. Social Security and food stamps offer a safety net. Roads allow us to get from one place to another. When the economy takes a turn for the worse, government policy can help lift it out of recession. Without government spending, too few of the public goods and services that we rely on would be produced. Some would not be produced at all.

The public sector also gives people jobs. In 1997, national, state, and local governments employed more than 21 million people, or about 15% of the work force. Public employment often provides women and people of color with better job opportunities than the private sector does.

Knickerbocker

Government spending and GDP in 1998 (in billions of $)

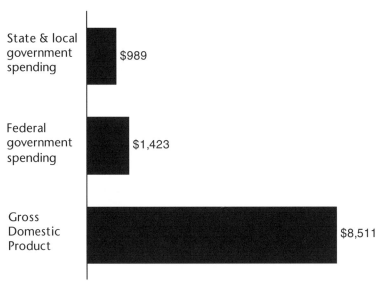

State & local government spending — $989

Federal government spending — $1,423

Gross Domestic Product — $8,511

5.2 Government Spending Elsewhere

Knickerbocker

Governments come in all shapes and sizes, some bigger than others. The U.S. has one of the smallest public sectors of any industrialized country. In 1997, government outlays amounted to 32% of American GDP, compared to 43% in Canada, 54% in France, and 62% in Sweden.

The size of the public sector is less important than its ability to deliver. Sure, the U.S. government spends a smaller proportion of its GDP than Canada, but 16% of Americans lack health insurance. In Canada, everyone is covered, with lower per capita medical care costs. Government spending on education, infrastructure, research, and family welfare can improve a country's competitive position in the global marketplace.

Priorities vary widely from country to country. In the U.S., the military chews up a much larger portion of federal dollars than in other developed countries, which spend more on social services and economic security.

Government spending as a percentage of GDP in selected countries in 1997

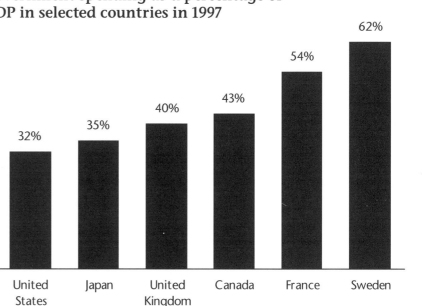

United States	Japan	United Kingdom	Canada	France	Sweden
32%	35%	40%	43%	54%	62%

5.3 Where Federal Dollars Go

Picture your tax dollar snipped into pieces of different sizes that show how the federal government actually spends it. About one-third goes to Social Security and Medicare; another third to the employees and resources that keep government programs humming; and one-sixth to the military. The remaining 15% pays interest on the national debt.

After the cold war, military spending shrank as a fraction of total spending. Back in the early days of the Vietnam War, the military absorbed close to half of federal outlays. In 1988, the year before the Berlin Wall fell, military spending still accounted for 27% of expenditures, but dropped to 16% by 1998. The money saved (the "peace dividend") went to support Social Security and Medicare, and to maintain human and physical resources in the public sector.

In the 1980s, high levels of borrowing pushed up the size of the national debt. The amount that the government borrows has dropped in recent years, but the debt remains. As a result, interest payments still account for a major part of federal spending.

Components of the federal budget

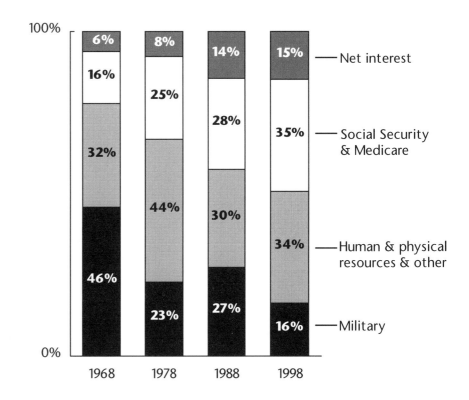

5.4 The Fate of Social Spending

Social spending hasn't fared well over the past two decades. Even with military cutbacks, expenditures on many social programs have dropped as a fraction of all federal outlays. In 1998, Uncle Sam spent proportionately less on education, training, employment, community development, and the environment than in 1980.

The federal government has directed a small fraction of its money towards maintaining a social safety net for Americans who fall on hard times. Spending on housing, food, and unemployment assistance fell from 6.4% of all outlays in 1980 to 5.3% in 1998.

On the other hand, due to rapidly increasing medical costs and an aging population, health-care expenditures have more than doubled over the same period.

Pressures to balance the budget and rein in government spending often target social spending first. Higher mandatory payments, such as interest on the national debt and Social Security obligations, have put many programs on the chopping block.

Selected social spending programs as a percentage of all federal outlays

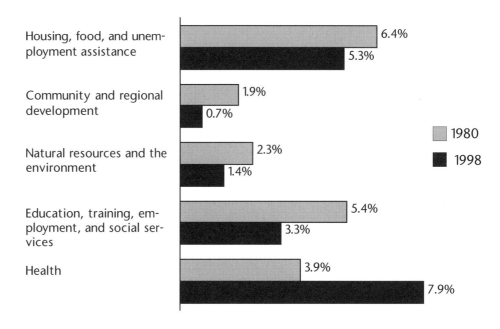

5.5 Stealth Bombers Don't Trickle Down

Spending billions of dollars on stealth bombers and cruise missiles to keep foreign menaces at bay might not be the most effective way to bolster American well-being. Investing the money in under-funded schools and programs to keep kids out of poverty could yield higher returns. But transforming military pri-orities into social ones can be tricky; the military-industrial complex still wields enormous power.

Military spending has fallen as a por-tion of the total budget, but the Pentagon still claims a substantial share. Over the years, many industries, such as ship-building, aircraft, and communications equipment, became overly dependent on the government for their sales. The conversion of these industries to civilian production has been slow and uneven. The ability of particular interest groups to lobby for their seat on the defense spending "gravy train" has blocked more far-reaching transformations.

Richard Mock

The costs of military and social programs

Military Program	Cost	Social Program
1 attack submarine	$2.3 billion	Head Start for 500,000 kids
1 F-22 bomber	$161 million	Pell grants for 100,000 students
1 Army division in Europe	$2.0 billion	Funding for 50,000 new teachers

5.6 Policing the World

Playing cop requires new strategies in the post-Cold War era. Instead of prepping for a massive battle between two superpowers, the U.S. Department of Defense has shifted gears, preparing to fight two smaller wars at the same time. It's no great bargain; the U.S. continues to spend more on its military than any other country in the world.

These days the American military outspends the Russians by a factor of nearly 4, China by a factor of 7, and Germany by 10. The combined military spending of so-called trouble spots—Iran, Iraq, Libya, and North Korea—doesn't even account for one-fifteenth of the U.S. military budget.

Cuts in military spending would not seriously imperil national security or the operations of international peacekeeping forces. But they would threaten industries and congressional districts that have come to depend on defense expenditures.

Military budgets, in billions ($1998)

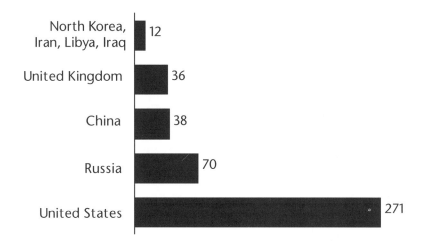

North Korea, Iran, Libya, Iraq	12
United Kingdom	36
China	38
Russia	70
United States	271

Nicole Hollander

5.7 Back in the Black

For the first time in nearly 30 years, the U.S. government has more money than it knows what to do with. These extra funds have sparked numerous debates in Congress and the White House. Should the surplus be used to bolster Social Security or give Americans a tax cut?

When the government spends more than it receives in taxes, it runs a budget deficit and must borrow to make up the difference. When revenues outpace spending, the federal budget runs a surplus. The largest deficits in recent decades occurred in the 1980s when Cold War military spending pushed the country deeper into debt. Only in the second half of the 1990s has borrowing dropped significantly.

Deficits and surpluses can be either good or bad. When growth slows down and unemployment creeps up, deficits increase spending power and give the economy a boost. As things improve, the government can pay back the borrowed money. Where these public dollars go is important. Many economists argue that programs that redistribute income, such as unemployment benefits and anti-poverty programs, boost growth as much as tax cuts do.

r. jay. magill

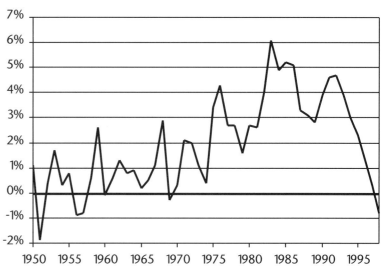

Deficit as a percentage of GDP, 1950-98

5.8 Borrowed Money

Imagine that America has one big credit card. Whenever spending plans go over budget, the government just charges the difference, adding the shortfall to what it already owes. For over 25 years, the U.S. has done just that. Public borrowing has dropped in recent years, but the debt from all those budget deficits remains outstanding.

In 1998, the national debt was about $5.5 trillion, or 65% of GDP. America actually owed more, relative to GDP, in the years following World War II. Stronger economic growth from 1950 to 1980 helped reduce the burden. But the 1980s witnessed a resurgence of borrowing.

Debt in itself is not bad. If public borrowing finances productive investment in education and infrastructure, it can pay off. But unproductive spending won't help the economy: a large debt diverts public spending into interest payments.

Gross federal debt as a percentage of GDP, 1950-98

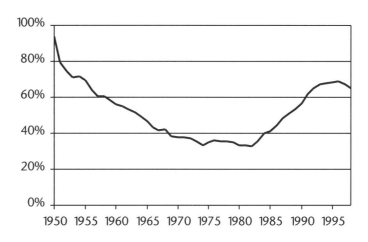

93

5.9 Who Pays the Taxes?

Images of long IRS forms and endless tax tables leap to mind. But income taxes account for less than half of all government revenues. Taxes come from many other sources. Social Security taxes are deducted from paychecks. Corporations pay taxes on their profits. And the government collects excise taxes on the sale of goods such as gasoline, alcohol, and cigarettes.

The relative importance of these different sources has changed over time. Income taxes account for slightly more of the total today than they did in 1960s. Corporate taxes shrank from 23% of all taxes in 1960 to just 11% in 1998. And excise taxes fell from 13% to 3% over the same time period.

Social Security taxes have become much more prominent. They now account for 33% of all federal taxes, up from 16% in 1960. As more women entered the work force, and as baby boomers became adults, more people began paying into Social Security.

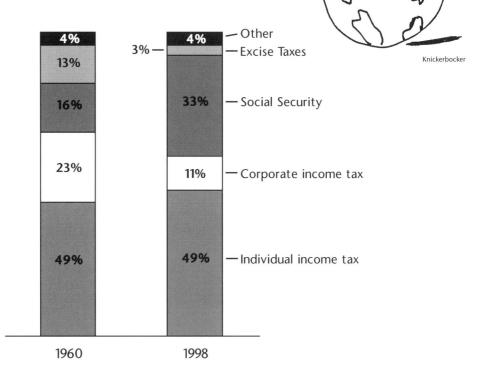

Sources of federal receipts, 1960 and 1998

1960	1998	
4%	4%	— Other
13%	3% —	— Excise Taxes
16%	33%	— Social Security
23%	11%	— Corporate income tax
49%	49%	— Individual income tax

Knickerbocker

5.10 Unfair Shares

In the U.S., the poorest families pay a larger share of their income in state and local taxes than the richest families do. In 1995, the bottom fifth of non-elderly married couples paid 12.5% of their incomes in sales, income, and property taxes. The richest 1% paid only 7.9%.

When a tax takes a bigger piece out of low incomes than high incomes, it's termed regressive. Both sales and property taxes fall into this category. The income tax works in the opposite direction, taking a larger share from the wealthy than from the poor.

State and local governments depend mostly on property and sales taxes.

No wonder many more affluent voters support moving funding responsibilities to the state and local level. It would save them money. Others argue for a federal "flat tax" in which everyone pays the same percentage. That too would make the U.S. tax system more regressive.

U.S. average state & local taxes in 1995 as a share of family income (for non-elderly married couples)

Income Group	Lowest 20%	Top 1%
Sales & Excise Taxes	6.7%	1.1%
Property Taxes	4.5%	1.9%
Income Taxes	1.3%	5.0%
Total	12.5%	7.9%

5.11 Taxing Business

Individuals are shouldering a heavier share of the tax bill in the U.S. while corporations are getting off more lightly. In 1960, individual payments made up 60% of total receipts while corporate taxes accounted for 23%. By 1998, the amount individuals paid had grown to a weighty 81% while corporations contributed only 11%.

Businesses depend on government services to operate. They need well-maintained roads, infrastructure, and an educated work force. They also need laws to enforce contracts and property rights. Government policies that support a stable economic environment allow firms to seize investment opportunities and maintain profitability.

Corporations argue that lower taxes encourage investment. When they get a free ride, however, individual taxpayers pick up the tab.

Tom Tomorrow

Tax receipts, by source, 1960-98

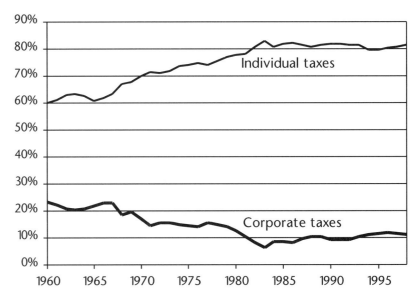

5.12 Buying Favors

Getting what you want from government can be a matter of knowing which palms to grease. Each year, special-interest groups spend tons of money to influence national legislation and spending priorities.

In 1997, the biggest spenders on lobbying services were the American Medical Association and tobacco producer Philip Morris. In both cases, congressional priorities on managed care and teenage smoking shifted. The third-biggest spender, Bell Atlantic, secured federal approval for its merger with NYNEX despite earlier legislation intended to increase competition in telecommunications.

High levels of spending to influence legislative outcomes can slow down important social reforms and distort public priorities.

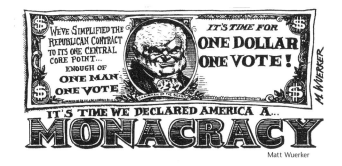

Matt Wuerker

Interest Group	Policy Issue	Political Spending 1997-98	Outcomes
Tobacco Industry	437,700 smoking-related deaths per year	$44 million	Bill to curb teen smoking stalled in Senate (1998)
Gun Rights	School shootings	$5 million	Child-Access Prevention Amendment tabled (1998)
Beer, Wine & Liquor Industry	Drunk drivers cause over 16,000 deaths per year	$12 million	Amendment to lower legal blood-alcohol level passed by Senate but not House (1998)
Health Insurance Industry	Patients concerned about quality of care from managed-care networks.	$87 million	Major providers have banded together to fight regulation and extension of patients' rights

5.13 Declining Democracy

Democracy doesn't work unless citizens speak up. However, a large fraction of Americans choose to remain silent when election day rolls around. In the 1964 presidential election, 62% of those eligible voted. In 1996, turnout slipped to less than half of registered voters.

Other countries enjoy higher rates of participation. In major 1996 elections, 87% of eligible voters in Italy and 60% of voters in Japan turned out, compared to only 49% in the U.S.

Maybe people feel that money speaks louder than votes when it comes to influencing government priorities. In 1997, national lobbying was a $1.26 billion industry, spending $2.4 million for each member of Congress.

Most Americans have a hard time keeping up with the influence industry. About 80% make no campaign contributions whatsoever. Of those individuals who do donate, 90% are white, 80% are men, and 46% make more than $250,000 a year.

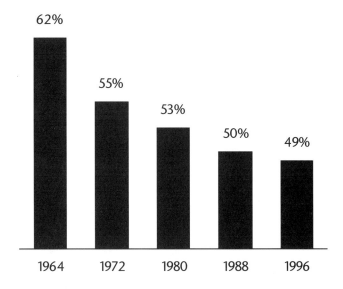

Turnout in selected U.S. presidential elections, 1964-96

1964	1972	1980	1988	1996
62%	55%	53%	50%	49%

5.14 Corporate Welfare

Estimates of the amount of money that the federal government doles out in "Aid to Dependent Corporations" range from $75 billion to $200 billion a year. The conservative Cato Foundation came up with the smaller number by defining corporate welfare as "any government spending program that provides unique benefits or advantages to specific companies or industries." A broader definition including tax loopholes as well as subsidies adds up to more than twice as much.

In March of 1999, the Congressional Progressive Caucus published a list of the "Fifteen Most Wanted" corporate subsidies that illustrates some of the specific programs they would like to eliminate. Five particularly interesting ones are listed here.

'Deserving Businesses'
"The Undeserving Poor"

THERE, THERE... IT'S A DOG EAT DOG WORLD. TO BE COMPETITIVE YOU'LL NEED THESE SUBSIDIES, TRADE POLICIES, AND OF COURSE SOME TAX BREAKS...

THANKS ALOT

GET A JOB PAL! DON'T YOU SEE IF I HELP YOU OUT, YOU'LL LOSE ALL SELF RESPECT, MORAL FORTITUDE, AND YOUR WILL TO WORK?!

WAP WAP

THANKS ALOT

GOVERNMENT'S HELPING HAND...

The five most colorful corporate welfare programs of 1999

GRAND CAYMAN COPOUT Poor regulation that allows U.S.-based multinational corporations to minimize taxes.	$12.2 billion
WARFARE WELFARE Grants, subsidies and tax breaks for arms-exporting companies.	$7.6 billion
SOAK THE TAXPAYER Subsidies of irrigation water.	$3.0 billion
GOLDEN GIVEAWAYS Failure to collect royalties on minerals extracted from public lands, and other loopholes for mining companies.	$1.0 billion
COWBOY SOCIALISM Failure to charge 100% pay-as-you-go grazing fees.	$200 million

5.15 Is Social Security Going Broke?

Are aging baby boomers going to break the Social Security bank? Our public retirement system taxes the people who are currently working to pay benefits to support the elderly and disabled. As the average age of the U.S. population rises, current contributions will have to support a growing number of retirees.

The Social Security program grew rapidly in the years following World War II, from 1.9% of federal outlays in 1950 to 23% in 1998. Most of this growth occurred in the first two decades. In fact, since 1973 increases in government resources have kept pace with Social Security spending.

Today Social Security helps more than 40 million retired and disabled persons. Current projections show that the current system could face a shortfall in 2032. But these estimates use conservative growth and budget forecasts. Whether Social Security will run into trouble depends on actual economic performance over the next three decades, as well as small adjustments in tax and benefit rates. The Social Security system may be old, but it's still pretty healthy.

Social Security spending as a percentage of total government outlays, 1950-99

5.16 Social Security or Insecurity?

Many policy makers argue that it's time to end Social Security as we know it. A system of private savings could replace the current pay-as-you-go system. But is this really a good idea?

- Social Security provides a predictable stream of lifetime benefits to retirees. In 1996, it was the primary source of income for 66% of recipients. In contrast, earnings from private accounts depend on the level of past savings and uncertain returns on each individual's investment.

- Moving from a pay-as-you-go system to private accounts would require substantial public resources because of the need to support current retirees while building up additional savings. Tax hikes, reducing benefits to the elderly, or increasing the national debt would be necessary to fund the switch.

- The current arrangement replaces a larger share of past earnings for people with low incomes than for high-income recipients. In 1996, Social Security kept 41% of the elderly out of poverty. Without such a system in place, privatizing social security could boost income inequality.

Tom Tomorrow

Chapter 6 **Welfare and Education**

Russell Christian

The ultimate test of an economy is whether or not it can give everyone a decent chance of prosperity. The United States doesn't score as high on this test as it used to. Income inequality has increased, more children live in poverty, and housing has become less affordable. Education is increasingly necessary to get ahead, but its growing costs have kept many from moving forward.

Family incomes increased steadily between 1950 and the mid-1970s. Since then, only married couples with a wife in the paid labor force have managed to boost their median income. Chart 6.1 shows that mothers on their own remain economically disadvantaged. While families at the top have seen their incomes rise, the bottom 40% of households have received a declining share of the total (see Chart 6.2).

What does poverty really mean? Nobody is very happy with the standard definition, which, as Chart 6.3 points out, overestimates economic privation in some ways and underestimates it in others. Chart 6.4 indicates that some groups are much more vulnerable to poverty—people of color and families raising children. Chart 6.5 traces poverty trends among children and the elderly. While the expansion of Social Security has reduced the fraction of the elderly who are poor, the number of poor children has grown in recent years. Chart 6.6 describes the social impact of child poverty.

Some people argue that the poor get too much assistance, creating a "culture of poverty." But as Chart 6.7 shows, most government transfers go to the affluent, not the needy. True, only the poor get welfare. Everyone else gets entitlements, subsidies, and tax breaks. Poor people will get even less help in the future. Chart 6.8 points out that "workfare" programs have replaced welfare programs, increasing the economic risks that poor families face. Where is it all headed? Chart 6.9 emphasizes that we don't know enough about what happens to families who leave the welfare rolls—many could be slipping through the cracks.

The decline in welfare programs has increased the lines at food pantries, soup kitchens, and shelters. Chart 6.10 outlines how the composition of people seeking assistance has changed. Meeting basic needs has become more difficult. As Chart 6.11 shows, the amount of affordable housing on the market has fallen. A decline in the amount of accessible housing contributes to a rise in homelessness. Families often find themselves out on the street: children represent 25% of the homeless population. Access to emergency shelters remains inadequate as nearly one third of families seeking shelter are turned away (Chart 6.12). And Chart 6.13 shows how the costs of another basic need—child care—consume a large portion of poor families' earnings.

The quality of education kids in the United States receive often depends on where they live. Chart 6.14 demonstrates that affluent regions spend much more per student than poor ones do. In addition, the price tag on a university education has been going up. Chart 6.15 tracks the increases for both private and public colleges. Financial aid hasn't grown enough to compensate. As Chart 6.16 shows, a larger fraction of individuals from wealthier families attend college these days than in the past. For poorer households, there has been no change.

6.1 Family Income

Many families are working harder and harder, yet barely maintaining their standard of living. Family incomes haven't increased much since the 1970s except for married couples with a wife in the paid labor force.

Worst off are families maintained by women alone, many of which live in poverty. In recent years, the number of families in this category has increased, pulling average family income down.

Growing differences in family structure have contributed to increases in income inequality: Two-earner families without children have more money to spend on luxuries than do single mothers who are struggling to combine paid work with family responsibilities.

Married women, entering the labor force in increasing numbers, have helped increase incomes for dual-earner families. But these families have additional expenses, such as child care, that offset some of the gains.

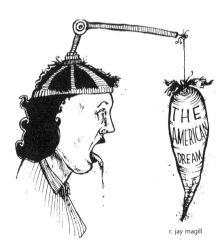

r. jay magill

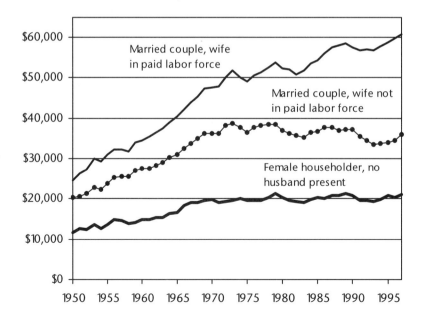

Median family income, 1950-97 ($1997)

Married couple, wife in paid labor force

Married couple, wife not in paid labor force

Female householder, no husband present

6.2 Low-Income Households Get a Smaller Share

The rich keep on getting richer. Almost any way you measure it, the gulf between top and bottom has widened in recent years. One of the most vivid indicators is the increased share of all income enjoyed by the top 5% of all households.

Differences in buying power have always been immense, with the top 5% claiming a bigger hunk of all household income than the bottom 40%. But today's disparities are so great that even Business Week suggests that the growing gap between rich and poor may be problematic. Harvard economist Richard Freeman asks if we are moving toward an apartheid economy.

Inequality increases social stresses, contributing to higher crime rates and a sense of insecurity at work. Inequality among children, in particular, violates basic principles of equal opportunity for all. Of course, inequality does offer some benefits for those at the top—it lowers the relative cost of hiring gardeners, maids and nannies.

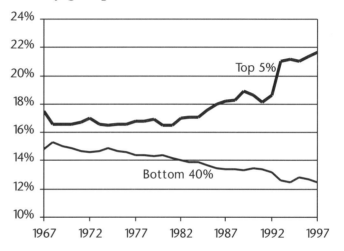

Shares of total household income received by groups of households

Nicole Hollander

6.3 Defining Poverty

The poverty line, designated by the U.S. Census Bureau, varies according to family size and composition. In 1998, it was $16,450 for a 4-person family—less than a third of the median income for married-couple families.

- Defined in the 1960s as the amount of money required for a subsistence diet multiplied by 3, the poverty line is updated yearly to account for inflation.

- Many experts argue that the poverty line is outmoded because food costs are a smaller share of family budgets today—rent and transportation costs have increased. Another problem is that the focus on income ignores the value of noncash transfers such as Food Stamps and Medicaid.

- The poverty line also fails to take into account the costs of child care for working parents. Families in which parents work for pay need more income in order to maintain the same standard of living as families in which a mother devotes more time to household tasks.

the poverty-level food pyramid

6.4 The Likelihood of Being Poor

Poverty threatens some people far more than others. In 1997, 27% of African Americans and Latinos had incomes below the poverty line, compared to 11% of whites.

Whatever their race or background, families with children are the most vulnerable. About 46% of families with children under 18 maintained by women alone had incomes under the poverty line.

Many families are poor despite the fact that they have members who work full-time. The current federal minimum wage of $5.15 adds up to annual wages of $10,712. Even when the value of the Earned Income Tax Credit for two children is added in, there's no way a single wage earner can keep a family of four out of poverty. Whether a married couple can succeed with both partners working for pay depends on the cost and availability of child care.

Education makes a big difference—most working families above the poverty line have at least one parent with a high school diploma.

People living in poverty in 1997

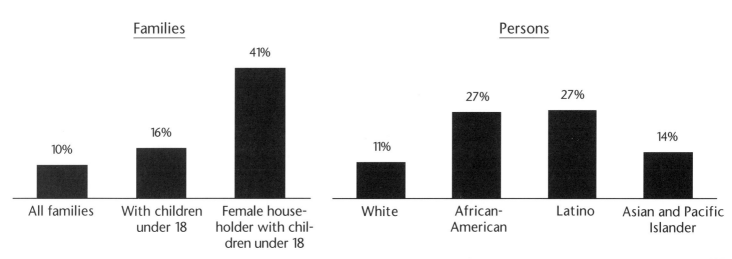

Families

- All families: 10%
- With children under 18: 16%
- Female householder with children under 18: 41%

Persons

- White: 11%
- African-American: 27%
- Latino: 27%
- Asian and Pacific Islander: 14%

6.5 Poverty Among Children and the Elderly

Many of the elderly remain poor, but as a group they are better off than children, whose overall poverty rate increased from 17% in 1975 to 20% in 1997. Social Security has done a relatively good job. Without the income it provides, about half of all Americans over 65 today would live in poverty.

Many children are poor because they live in families that receive little or no financial support from an adult male. Government assistance is stingy. Even those families eligible for Temporary Assistance for Needy Families (TANF) receive only limited assistance.

Why can't we do better? Other countries, including Canada, Australia, Sweden, Germany, the Netherlands, and France, provide a genuine social safety net. The poverty rate for their children is about one-third that in the U.S.; for their elderly, the poverty rate is one-fourth as high.

Percentage of children and elderly in poverty

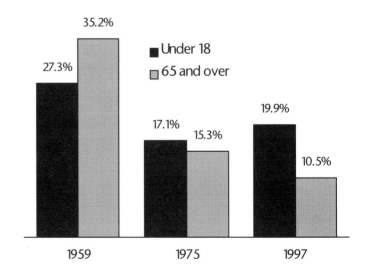

■ Under 18
▨ 65 and over

1959: 27.3% / 35.2%
1975: 17.1% / 15.3%
1997: 19.9% / 10.5%

6.6 Poverty Hurts Kids

- Poverty rates among children vary dramatically among states. In 1997, one-third of all children living in Mississippi lived in poverty, compared to only one-tenth in Wisconsin. Almost 20% of low-income children in Texas lacked a usual source of health care, compared to only 3% in Minnesota.

- Poor children face serious risks. Relative to non-poor children, they are 6.8 times as likely to be victims of child abuse and neglect, 3.5 times as likely to suffer lead poisoning, and 1.7 times as likely to die.

- Poverty in early childhood has a negative effect on children's future educational achievement.

- Children in poverty are more likely to be separated from their parents. The rate of children living in foster care has increased from 4.2 in 1982 to 7.3 in 1996.

Tom Tomorrow

6.7 Handouts for the Affluent

Most folks think that social spending is intended primarily for the poor. Not so. Direct spending and tax expenditures (exclusions from taxable income that lower tax revenues) transfer far more money to the affluent. Only low-income families are eligible for programs such as Medicaid, Food Stamps, the Earned Income Tax Credit, or Aid to Families with Dependent Children (recently replaced by Temporary Assistance for Needy Families).

By contrast, Medicare provides health benefits to citizens over age 65 regardless of income. Highly paid workers are likely to enjoy employer contributions to health insurance and pension costs, which are excluded from taxation.

The deductibility of mortgage interest on owner-occupied homes is a particularly striking case. Since few poor people own expensive homes, they seldom benefit. But this deduction is worth, on average, about $5,000 a year to taxpayers making more than $200,000.

Government benefits and tax expenditures in 1996 (in billions of $1996)

Matt Wuerker

For persons with limited income		For persons regardless of income	
Medicaid	$159.4	Medicare and exclusion of employer contributions for health insurance.	$264.5
Food Stamps, AFDC, and earned income tax credit	$56.1	Tax exclusion for pension contributions and earnings	$56.5
Low-income housing credit	$15.0	Deductibility of mortgage interest on owner-occupied homes	$47.5

6.8 Welfare Farewell

In 1996, Congress replaced Aid to Families with Dependent Children (AFDC) with Temporary Assistance for Needy Families (TANF).

- TANF requires recipients to find employment or be placed in unpaid jobs for 20 hours a week as quickly as possible and sets a maximum lifetime limit of 60 months on receipt of public assistance. Unlike AFDC, it offers no guarantee that families with young children under the poverty line will receive public assistance. Federal funding is capped through 2002.

- Between August 1996 and December 1998, the number of families receiving assistance fell 37%. Much of this decline was due to declining unemployment rates that made it easier for women to find jobs, but changes in welfare rules probably also played a role.

- Some recipients were able to find jobs, but many others were terminated because they failed to comply with rules. New applications for public assistance have declined considerably.

- National survey data show that only a small percentage of mothers are able to find jobs that pay enough to allow them to live above the poverty line. Moreover, few of their employers offer health insurance. For most families, continued eligibility for Medicaid is only temporary.

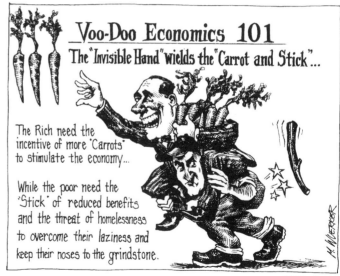

Matt Wuerker

6.9 From Welfare to What?

Major changes in the way public assistance is administered, along with enormous variation among state policies, make it difficult to assess the merits of welfare reform. Here are some of the questions and concerns that critics have raised:

- Work requirements, especially those that entail many hours of community service in return for public assistance, may force individuals to work for below-minimum wages.

- A college degree is the best ticket out of long-run poverty. Yet most states discourage recipients from pursuing a college degree by refusing to count this activity as a substitute for work. Job-training programs are also quite limited.

- Many single mothers may be seriously constrained by lack of affordable child care, or forced to resort to extremely low-quality child-care arrangements.

- What happens to families who get kicked off the rolls? Few states have set up adequate monitoring systems to study the consequences of their policies. Most of the families able to make a transition from welfare to work may have already done so. As state time limits begin to kick in, some families may run into serious trouble.

- What will happen if we enter a recession and unemployment rates go up? Many people seeking work will be unable to find it, yet will have no recourse to further public assistance.

112

6.10 Bare Cupboards

Welfare reform has changed the face of lines at soup kitchens and charitable food pantries.

Working mothers are increasingly likely to show up asking for assistance. Many are afraid to apply for Food Stamps out of fear that it might reduce their eligibility for future assistance.

In 1997, visits to charitable food programs increased 15% over the previous year.

In New York City, welfare officials eager to cut the rolls actually delayed Food Stamp applications and directed needy individuals to private food pantries (a Federal judge later ruled this practice illegal). In Wisconsin, families who left the welfare rolls were 50% more likely to report that they didn't have enough money for food.

The extent of hunger depends on how you define it. In 1997, more than 30 million Americans were unable to buy food for themselves and their children for some part of each month.

Characteristics of individuals seeking assistance from food pantries, soup kitchens, and shelters in 1997

r. jay magill

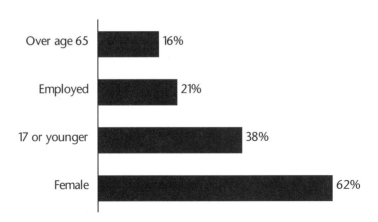

Over age 65 — 16%
Employed — 21%
17 or younger — 38%
Female — 62%

6.11 Searching for Shelter

When the economy booms, rents go up. Poor people must spend a larger proportion of their income on shelter, and not all can afford to pay. Some end up on the streets.

The gap between the number of needy families (those earning less than $12,000 a year) and affordable apartments (those which rented for less than $300 per month) has increased significantly over this period of time. As Andrew Cuomo, Secretary of Housing and Urban Development, put it, "there are a lot more $6-an-hour jobs than $6-an-hour apartments."

Although about 15 million households now qualify for federal housing assistance, only about 4.5 million families get it. In New York, the average wait for subsidized housing is 8 years. In Los Angeles, the average wait for a voucher subsidy is 10 years.

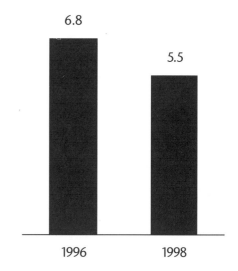

Number of housing units renting for less than $300 (in millions)

6.8 — 1996
5.5 — 1998

6.12 Mean Streets

Families living in comfortable neighbhorhoods may not see it, but homelessness remains a serious problem in this country.

- On a given night, between 600,000 and 700,000 people are homeless.

- Requests for emergency shelter increased 15% for families in 1998.

- Nearly one-third of families seeking shelter were turned away for lack of space.

- Children represent about 25% of the homeless population. Another 20% are individuals who are employed either full- or part-time.

- Many efforts to address this problem focus on emergency measures rather than root causes. A recent study of homeless families in New York City suggests that the real problem is the city's scarcity of subsidized housing.

WHY RICH PEOPLE DON'T SLEEP ON THE SIDE WALK

RICH PEOPLE DON'T SLEEP ON THE SIDEWALK BECAUSE THEY ARE POLITE AND CONSIDERATE, AND KNOW THAT THEIR BED-STEADS WOULD CAUSE AN UN-NECESSARY INTERRUPTION TO PEDESTRIAN TRAFFIC.

6.13 Kid Care

To pay their bills, many parents have to work harder and longer. That means they have to find someone else to look after their kids.

- The costs of child care are a particularly serious problem for low-income families. Families with preschoolers who had incomes below the poverty line in 1993 spent an average of 18% of their income on child care, compared to 7% for those above the poverty line.

- Many low-wage earners work irregular hours or at night, a factor that makes it especially difficult for them to find child care.

- Middle class families receive rebates for their child-care costs through the Dependent Child Care Tax Credit system, while low-income families who owe little or no tax do not benefit.

- Current child-care subsidies for low-income families are inadequate. Only about one out of ten eligible children receive such subsidies.

- The quality of care varies widely. One study found that 13% of regulated and 50% of non-regulated family child-care providers were inadequate. In general, states with stronger licensing requirements have better-quality child care.

6.14 Poor Schools for Poor Kids

Most public schools in the U.S. rely heavily on local property taxes, which leads to considerable inequality in funding. In some states, affluent school districts spend 9 times as much per pupil as do poorer districts.

While the U.S. Constitution makes few references to education, many state constitutions promise educational opportunity for all citizens. Reformers have successfully won lawsuits forcing states to reduce funding inequality in more than 16 states. In most cases, court-ordered changes have significantly increased per-student funding in poor districts.

Even if further initiatives succeed, however, differences across states remain extreme. In 1995-96, students in New Jersey enjoyed a level of expenditures more than two times higher than that of Alabama.

Differences in per-pupil expenditures across states, 1995-96

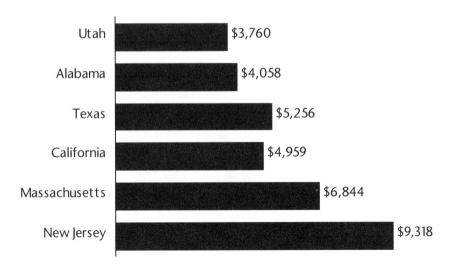

Utah	$3,760
Alabama	$4,058
Texas	$5,256
California	$4,959
Massachusetts	$6,844
New Jersey	$9,318

Matt Wuerker

6.15 The Price of College

Knickerbocker

Acollege diploma is worth at least its weight in gold. College graduates have a much higher chance than others of getting and keeping decent jobs. Unfortunately, the price of attendance keeps going up, especially for students attending private schools. Public universities have kept a better lid on, despite cutbacks in state funding. But many have been forced to hire more part-time faculty, increase class size, and defer maintenance on buildings in order to keep their costs down.

The price that students pay is actually far less than the cost of providing the services they receive. Subsidies to college education, including financial aid, average about $8,200 per student. The average student pays about $3,800 a year and gets the benefit of about $12,000 in educational expenditures. The average subsidy is about the same at private institutions—but both price and cost are higher.

The social and economic distance between students attending relatively cheap public institutions and those at private schools is increasing.

Average price of attendance, public and private universities, 1964-65 to 1996-97
(total tuition, room and board in $1997)

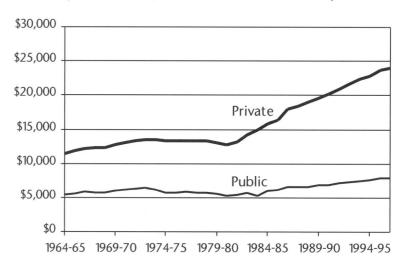

118

6.16 Who Graduates From College?

If everyone had equal access to a college education, family income wouldn't affect their chances of success. But affluent kids clearly have a big advantage, one that is increasing over time. In 1994, about 79% of children from families in the richest 25% had received a college degree by age 24, compared to 31% in 1979. Those from families in the poorest 25%, however, remained stuck at a much lower level of 8%.

Among other things, affluent families can help out more with college costs. According to one recent survey, college students from families with incomes of $100,000 or more received an average of $9,373 in gifts from their parents, compared to $2,825 from families with incomes under $20,000.

Financial aid significantly increases the likelihood that poor students will graduate from college. But direct grants for low-income families have declined substantially relative to tuition rates. "Need-blind" financial aid, once provided by many elite private schools to those who met their strict admissions criteria, is now less common.

Increased inequality of income among parents increases inequality of opportunities among children—and vice versa. Greater differences in the likelihood of graduating from college will further increase income inequality.

Percentage of individuals from rich and poor families receiving a college degree by age 24.

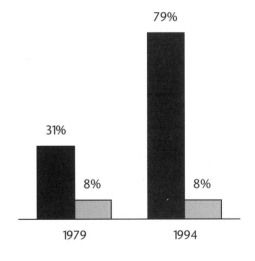

From richest 25% of families

From poorest 25% of families

Chapter 7 **Health**

Russell Christian

The U.S. health-care system has been sick for years, but political bickering and special interests continue to block an effective cure. The problems are chronic; many Americans lack health insurance, drug prices keep climbing, and the quality of care too often depends on a person's ability to pay.

Chart 7.1 tracks the trend in health spending in the United States and other industrialized countries. We used to spend about the same portion of our GDP on health services as other countries did. But since the 1980s, our outlays have increased at a much faster rate. Despite big expenditures, Americans live shorter lives than people in other developed countries, as Chart 7.2 documents.

Health care in this country is complicated and expensive. Employer-provided insurance, out-of-pocket payments, and government programs all help settle the bill. Chart 7.3 shows that government and business combined account for about two-thirds of health spending. Chart 7.4 points out that, despite programs such as Medicaid, rising health costs and lack of insurance mean that poor families spend a large share of their income on medical services.

The prices of health-related goods and services (pictured in Chart 7.5) have risen much more rapidly than the consumer price index. Chart 7.6 describes how declining hospital use has actually contributed to higher costs for each day a patient stays. Competing for customers, hospitals engage in a technological "arms race," acquiring expensive equipment instead of bidding down costs.

Pharmaceutical companies can charge extremely high prices for their products in order to protect their revenues. Chart 7.7 indicates how high prices translate into big profits. In addition, physicians can make so much more money in highly paid specialties that many are reluctant to enter general practice (Chart 7.8).

Low-income families are probably pretty sick and tired of feeling sick and tired. Chart 7.9 shows how the health status of poorer households fails to match that of richer people. Lack of access to medical insurance helps explain why less affluent families feel less healthy. Chart 7.10 points out that one-third of people with incomes below one and a half times the poverty line lack medical insurance.

The health-care system is rife with racial and ethnic inequalities. Chart 7.11 describes how many people of color lack health insurance—nearly one-third of all Latinos and one-fifth of all African Americans and Asian Americans. Children of color have a smaller chance of surviving to adulthood than white children. Chart 7.12 shows that the ratio of black infant deaths per 1,000 to white infant deaths per 1,000 increased significantly in the 1980s.

Growing health costs prompted policymakers to support an expansion in the number of providers who "manage" care. Chart 7.13 documents how the composition of health-care providers changed since 1980. Health Maintenance Organizations (HMOs) and Preferred Provider Organizations (PPOs) have eclipsed traditional fee-for-service arrangements. The shift ushered in numerous problems, as Chart 7.14 points out. Faced with pressures to maintain profitability, many HMOs are turning away patients, raising prices, or simply going out of business.

However pressing the need for reform in the United States, it is important to maintain an international perspective. Chart 7.15 reveals that many developing countries suffer from diseases that they have the know-how but not the money to control. The spread of HIV and AIDS is now one of the most serious public health problems in the world. Many poorer nations, particularly those in Africa, lack the resources to maintain effective prevention campaigns. Soaring death rates have a severe emotional and economic impact (Chart 7.16).

7.1 Hey, Big Spender

Throwing money at a problem doesn't necessarily make it go away. The U.S. spends far more of its gross domestic product on health care than other industrialized countries do, even though in 1997 over 43 million people—about 16% of the population—lacked medical insurance.

It's a story of excess and deprivation in which the failure to develop a well-coordinated health-care system plays a major role. Americans rely on a hodge-podge of private insurance, public assistance, and out-of-pocket payments that finances luxury treatments for some but begrudges basic care to others.

Doctors and hospitals are increasingly torn between the pressure to protect profits and the desire to provide decent health care. Many feel trapped in a system that often pits these objectives against each other.

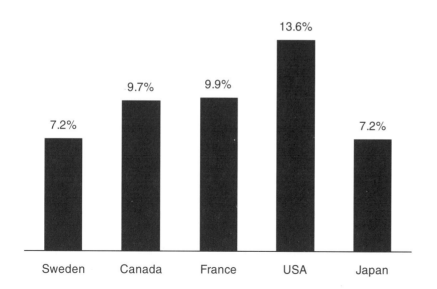

Health care spending as a percentage of GDP in 1995

Sweden	Canada	France	USA	Japan
7.2%	9.7%	9.9%	13.6%	7.2%

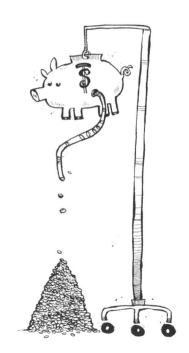

7.2 Spend More, Live Less

When it comes to staying healthy, Americans get less bang for their buck than citizens of other industrialized countries. Despite high levels of health spending per capita, people in the U.S. just don't live as long.

The U.S. lags behind most other highly developed countries in numerous indicators, including infant mortality and life expectancy. Why? Other countries provide basic health care for all their citizens, but the U.S. allocates services principally to those who can pay for them. Unequal access and the high cost of care add up to a less-healthy population.

Income inequality itself is stressful. A recent study of affluent countries showed that, all else being equal, greater inequality seems to lower life expectancy. No matter who you are, poverty is bad for your health.

Life expectancy and health spending in 1995

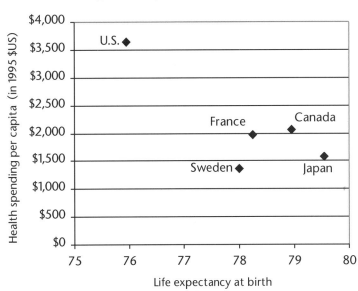

7.3 Look Who's Paying

Paying the bill for U.S. health care requires snatching a dollar here, a dollar there, out of many different pockets. About 61% of the population have some kind of employer-provided coverage. Others buy their own insurance or rely on government programs like Medicare.

Employers have been willing to provide medical benefits because these aren't taxed. $1,000 in health insurance is worth more to an employee than $1,000 in extra pay. However, rising health-care costs have caused many employers to cut back. Once benefits disappear, they seldom rematerialize. Despite good economic performance in the second half of the 1990s, employer coverage hasn't rebounded.

As the population ages, a larger number of people rely on Medicare and Medicaid to meet their needs. This trend helps explain why government's share of health spending has grown recently. Plus, because these programs have lower average overhead costs than private insurance, they offer a more efficient way of providing care.

Expenditures on health care by type of payer in 1995

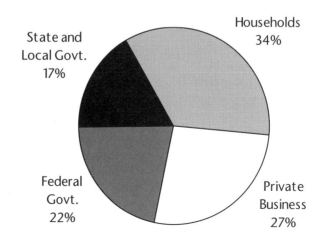

State and Local Govt. 17%

Households 34%

Federal Govt. 22%

Private Business 27%

7.4 Poor People Pay More

Unlike liposuction and face-lifts, most health services are necessities. When people get sick, they have no choice but to seek help, regardless of their income. As a result, poor families spend a larger part of their income on health care than wealthier households do.

In 1997, the poorest fifth of earners spent 30% of their before-tax income on medical care, but the top fifth paid only about 15%. Richer households generally receive high-quality care for their money while people lacking insurance typically face long lines in hospital emergency rooms. Many middle-class workers fear losing their insurance if they get laid off, and private insurers often refuse to enroll individuals with "pre-existing conditions."

Doctors, medicines, and insurance cost about the same if you are rich or poor. If the U.S. delivery system provided more publicly financed care, the burden could be more equally distributed. Risks could also be spread more evenly.

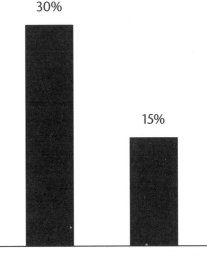

Health care spending as a percentage of before-tax income in 1997

7.5 The Unhealthy Cost of Care

Inflation has long been a fact of life in the U.S. But in recent years the price of medical care has gotten blown out of proportion. While consumer prices increased by about a factor of 4 between 1970 and 1996, the costs of medical care increased by a factor of seven. The upward path of health costs has leveled off somewhat in recent years, but many expect larger increases in the near future.

Technological change contributes to rapidly rising costs. But the fact that other countries have controlled expenses without sacrificing quality suggests that our health care system itself is ailing.

We need to diagnose, and cure, the high-cost fever that's plaguing hospitals, pharmaceutical companies, physicians, and insurance companies. Otherwise, the sight of our next medical bill could really make us sick.

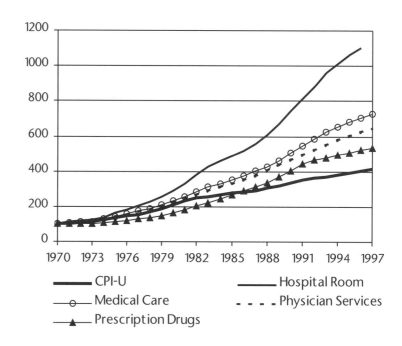

Price indices for medical costs, 1970-97 (1970=100)

Legend:
- CPI-U
- Medical Care
- Prescription Drugs
- Hospital Room
- Physician Services

7.6 A Day in the Hospital

Trips to the local hospital come with such hefty price tags these days that doctors prescribe them less. With rising costs, hospitals must vie for well-insured customers who can cover the bills.

As hospital stays get more expensive, insurers often only pay for a short, fixed period of more intensive care. The average hospital stay fell from 11.4 days in 1975 to only 7.5 days in 1996. When a patient leaves the hospital these days, family members often fill the gap, working long hours to provide necessary care.

Hospitals don't compete with each other by offering the lowest prices in town. Instead, they try to offer the most high-tech care available, getting caught up in a medical "arms race" that leads them to invest in more equipment than they can efficiently use.

Increased competitive pressures are driving non-profit and teaching hospitals out of business.

Nicole Hollander

Average cost per day to community hospitals, per patient (in $1997)

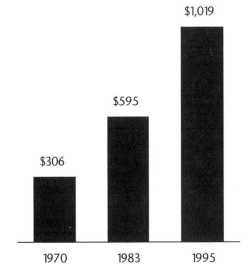

1970	1983	1995
$306	$595	$1,019

7.7 It Pays to Specialize

Imagine that you could double your income and pay off your staggering school loans simply by choosing one specialization over another within your career of choice. In the U.S., physicians face considerable financial pressures not to become general practitioners. No wonder America has a relative excess of specialists.

Between 1973 and 1996, general practitioners have seen their inflation-adjusted income drop slightly. Over the same period, incomes of surgeons, radiologists, and gynecologists increased between 8% and 20%. In 1996, over half of doctors in the bottom quarter of the pay scale were general practitioners, compared to only 20% of physicians in the top quarter.

The probability that a physician will work as an employee has increased in recent years. Managed care plans tend to tilt towards employing more primary-care providers to reduce costs, but doctors earn more by specializing and choosing self-employment. How these inconsistencies will be ironed out in the future remains to be seen.

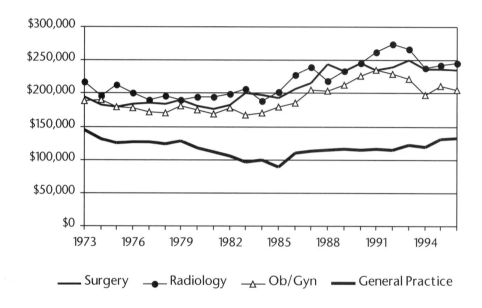

Physicians' median net income by specialization, 1973-96 ($1997)

—— Surgery —•— Radiology —△— Ob/Gyn —— General Practice

Knickerbocker

7.8 R_x = Big Bucks

There's a lot of money to be made in drugs. For the past forty years, the pharmaceutical industry has consistently enjoyed higher returns than almost any other industrial group. In 1997, returns on shareholder's equity for the Fortune 500 averaged 13%, while pharmaceuticals boasted a 39% return.

How do they do it? Mostly by keeping prices high. Monopolies on new drug production, aggressive lobbying of doc-tors to prescribe their products, and emphasis on brand names allow these corporations to maintain huge profit margins. In 1998, companies spent $10.8 billion in advertising to lure consumers away from cheaper generic drugs.

The elderly are particularly likely to feel the heavy burden of high medicine prices. Since Medicare doesn't cover pre-scriptions, out-of-pocket expenses for pharmaceuticals can eat up a large share of older American's fixed income.

In countries with a single payer health care system, the government ne-gotiates directly with drug companies, helping to keep a lid on prices.

Russell Christian

Return on shareholder's equity, 1961-98

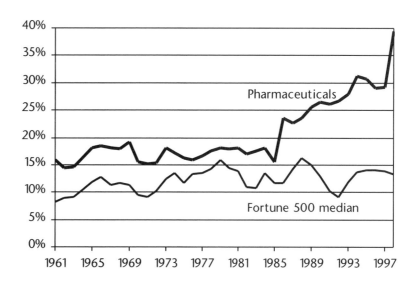

7.9 Earn More, Feel Better

Money might not buy happiness, but it sure can make you feel healthier. In 1997, one in four people with family incomes below $18,112 a year considered themselves in poor or fair health. Among those earning over $75,000, only one in twenty felt the same. Of this more affluent group, 41% reported excellent health, compared to only 20% of individuals from the low-income cluster.

Because many lower-income households lack affordable health insurance, they often postpone care until medical problems turn critical. In 1997, 30% of the uninsured did not receive the care they needed, and 55% postponed care because of lack of access.

Some people get caught in a health-poverty trap. Poor health makes it difficult to find and keep a well-paying job. But without that job, they can't get the health care they need.

Percentage of people reporting poor or fair health, by family income, in 1997

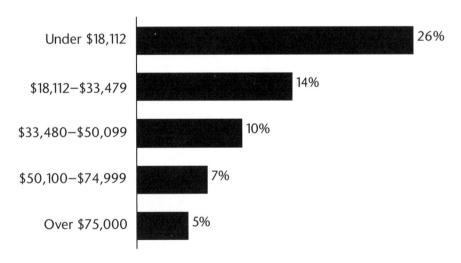

Under $18,112	26%
$18,112–$33,479	14%
$33,480–$50,099	10%
$50,100–$74,999	7%
Over $75,000	5%

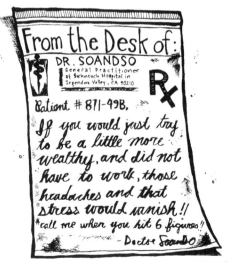

r. jay magill

7.10 Too Poor for Care

When poor people get sick, their options for help are limited. Many end up in the emergency room, taking whatever services they can get. Medicare provides assistance to those 65 years or older and Medicaid targets poor families, but eligibility is limited. In 1997, only 43% of poor people were covered by Medicaid at some time during the year.

In 1996, one third of all households with incomes below 150% of the poverty line had no medical coverage. Among families with incomes over twice the poverty threshold, only 7% lacked insurance. Many of the uninsured have jobs; in 1997, about half of all poor full-time workers lacked medical coverage.

Access to insurance varies from region to region. In 1997, Hawaii, Wisconsin, and Minnesota had the highest fraction of the population insured. States in the southwest with large Latino immigrant populations, including Texas, New Mexico, and Arizona, had the lowest rates of coverage.

Percentage of people under age 65 lacking health insurance by poverty status in 1996

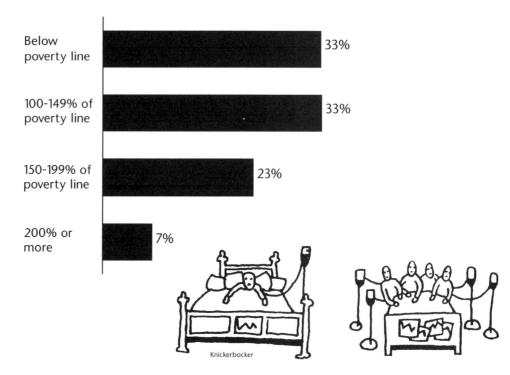

Below poverty line	33%
100-149% of poverty line	33%
150-199% of poverty line	23%
200% or more	7%

Knickerbocker

131

7.11 People of Color Lack Insurance

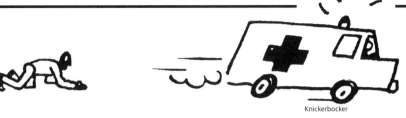

Knickerbocker

Since health care is costly, it's hardly surprising that groups with low average incomes have less of it. In 1997, 22% of African Americans, 21% of Asian Americans, and 34% of Latinos lacked insurance compared to 15% of whites. Differences are smaller for people living in poverty; among all racial and ethnic groups, roughly a third of the poor have no coverage.

Unequal access to medical care contributes to poor health for people of color. In 1996, life expectancy for African Americans was six years less than the U.S. average. And the death rate for Native Americans from diabetes was more than twice that for whites.

Both regional and historical factors help explain why Latinos are particularly likely to be uninsured. Often they have jobs with low pay and slim benefits. Also, many are immigrants who lack information about the U.S. health system and might be afraid to seek medical assistance if it means dealing with the authorities. 52% of all poor immigrants in the U.S. lack insurance.

Percentage of people in various racial and ethnic groups lacking health insurance in 1997

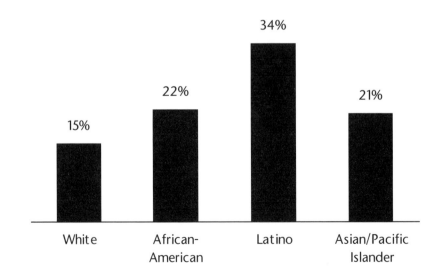

7.12 African-American Children at Greater Risk

Nothing highlights inequalities in the U.S. health care system more starkly than the disparities in infant mortality rates by race. The ratio of African-American to white infant mortality rates began to increase in 1974 and grew larger in the late 1980s and early 1990s.

In 1996, the infant mortality rate for African-American infants was 14.7 per 1,000 live births, compared to 6.1 for whites. African-American infants face the same risk of death as infants in much poorer countries, such as Bulgaria and Costa Rica. Some inner-city neighborhoods suffer from even worse odds.

Limited access to health insurance and prenatal care accounts for a large part of the problem. In 1996, 84% of all white mothers received prenatal care during the first trimester compared to 71% of African-American mothers. Growing inequality in the life chances of infants reflects the polarization of income in the economy as a whole.

Ratio of African-American infant mortality rate to white infant mortality rate, 1964-1996

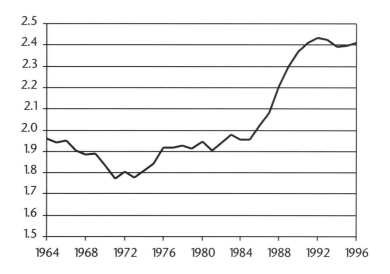

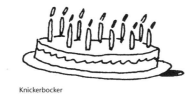

Knickerbocker

7.13 Managing Care

They wanted to cut U.S. health care costs. The operation seemed like a success at first, but the patient is looking pretty shaky. In 1980, conventional fee-for-service arrangements accounted for 92% of medical plans. By 1998, health maintenance organizations (HMOs) provided 52% of the total, as conventional plans shrank to 14%.

Unlike conventional coverage in which a patient chooses a provider and insurance pays the bill, HMOs charge a fixed fee and then contract with or directly employ providers. In contrast, a preferred provider organization (PPO) maintains a network of services but their fees are not fixed.

Profits play a larger role than ever before in almost every facet of health care. The profit motive compels providers to cut costs. But as competition intensifies, it also rewards bad behavior. HMOs can save money by dumping patients, pushing up fees, or lowering quality. Some are merging with bigger providers while others are simply going out of business, leaving patients frustrated and confused.

Health-care insurance enrollment

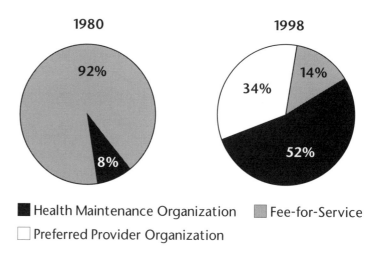

1980

1998

■ Health Maintenance Organization ■ Fee-for-Service
□ Preferred Provider Organization

Nicole Hollander

7.14 HMO Woes

For a while, Health Maintenance Organizations (HMOs) seemed like a solution to all our health care problems. Not any more.

- Many medical costs, such as drug prices, remain out of the control of HMOs. Unless such systemic problems are solved, many HMOs will either be forced to pass on costs or go bankrupt.

- Quality of services remains uneven across managed care providers. In July 1998, 50% of respondents to a *New York Times* poll thought that more managed care would harm quality. Only 32% thought HMOs improved care.

- Studies by the National Committee for Quality Assurance show that not-for-profit plans provide higher quality care than for-profit plans.

- Managed care can lead to reduced services for the poor and uninsured. In the past, hospitals subsidized uncompensated care by making insurers pay more. If managed care continues to grow, this practice will probably become less common.

Tom Tomorrow

135

7.15 Health Around the World

Knickerbocker

Health problems that are history in developed nations still ravage poorer countries, killing millions every year. Malaria, diarrhea, and dysentery run rampant in the less developed world. Each year 5 million people die of diarrhea, 3 million of them children.

Getting basic medical care poses huge challenges for people living in poor countries. For every 100,000 people, industrialized countries have 20 times more doctors and 30 times more nurses than the least-developed nations.

Air pollution kills about 2.7 million people each year; 90% of these deaths occur in poor countries. More than 1.3 million people worldwide lack access to safe drinking water and over 2.5 million lack adequate sanitation. Such underdevelopment is deadly. If everyone had safe water and basic sanitation, an estimated 2 million lives could be saved each year.

Health conditions in 1995

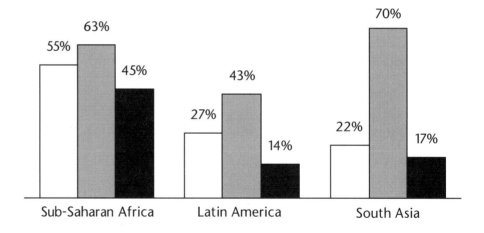

	Sub-Saharan Africa	Latin America	South Asia
% population without safe water	55%	27%	22%
% population without adequate sanitation	63%	43%	70%
% children under 1 year without measles immunization	45%	14%	17%

□ % population without safe water

▨ % population without adequate sanitation

■ % children under 1 year without measles immunization

7.16 AIDS

A persistent killer continues to stalk people in communities around the world. While AIDS can strike anyone, it mostly infects the young and the poor. Sub-Saharan Africa has been hit the worst, with an estimated 22.5 million adults and children living with HIV/AIDS. Cumulative deaths worldwide as of December 1998 totaled almost 14 million.

Since the disease strikes people in their most productive years, the economic consequences of HIV/AIDS are potentially enormous. For example, in Botswana, average life expectancy has been reduced by 20 years. This loss of life is devastating on a number of levels. It cripples a country's productive potential and raises the question of who will raise the next generation. In 1997 alone, AIDS orphaned 1.6 million children.

Poor countries bear a disproportionate burden of the epidemic. Expensive treatments allow people in rich nations to live longer, but the annual costs of medication for one person exceed the per-capita GDP of most developing countries.

Adults and children living with HIV/AIDS in 1998

Sub-Saharan Africa	22,500,000
Asia & the Pacific	7,272,000
Latin America & the Caribbean	1,730,000
North America	890,000
Western Europe	500,000
North Africa/ Middle East	210,000

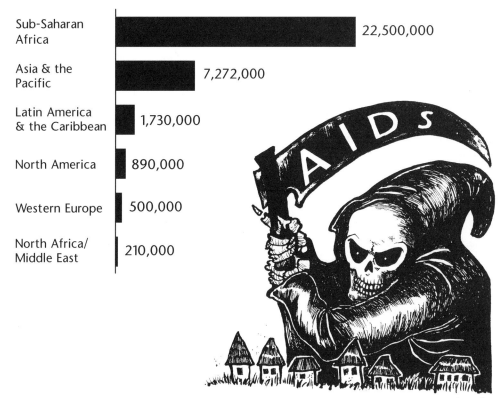

r. jay magill

137

Chapter 8 **Environment**

Russell Christian

From silent springs to nuclear winters, environmental hazards have become a perennial feature of the U.S. economic landscape. Clean air, good water, and stable ecosystems don't have obvious price tags, and it's difficult to measure their deterioration. Companies under pressure to maximize their profits are easily tempted to ignore the pollution they create if they aren't forced to clean it up. But the future of our economy depends heavily on the future of our ecosystem.

Environmentalists are often suspicious of an emphasis on growth—with good reason. Economists typically define growth simply in terms of what gets bought and sold, ignoring the value of assets outside the market economy. Chart 8.1 contrasts the growth of per-capita Gross Domestic Product (GDP) with a new measure called the Genuine Progress Indicator (GPI), which suggests that not much real progress has been made since 1973. Chart 8.2 estimates the value of all the services Mother Nature provides to keep our societies going, suggesting that we are all in her debt.

Among the many insults to our environment is toxic waste. Chart 8.3 documents some of the corporate sources of this problem. Meanwhile, households are generating more and more trash. Chart 8.4 shows that, despite significant efforts to recycle, solid waste is piling up. Some people are more affected by environmental hazards than others. Chart 8.5 offers evidence that people of color are especially likely to live in communities with high pollution levels. Chart 8.6 points out that improperly stored hazardous waste remains a public health threat throughout the country.

Despite growing public concern and new government programs, environmental problems remain widespread. Advances in some areas have been countervailed by reverses in others. Chart 8.7 explains that the growth in decentralized sources of pollution, such as fertilizer runoffs, has reversed earlier successes in improving water quality of rivers and streams.

Some policy-makers claim that environmental regulations destroy jobs. But as Chart 8.8 indicates, environment-friendly or "green" businesses actually create employment opportunities. Unfortunately, the backlash against environmentalism has made it difficult to increase or even maintain enforcement efforts. Chart 8.9 shows that the Environmental Protection Agency lacks the resources it needs to develop a truly effective environmental defense system. In some cases, market forces can help out. Carefully designed policies that require polluters to pay, but give them some flexibility in deciding how to pay, can have a positive impact, as Chart 8.10 explains.

A big challenge to sustainability comes from the profligate way our economy uses energy. Chart 8.11 shows that we drive more cars than anyone else, guzzling gas and generating exhaust fumes. The U.S. economy consumes a huge share of the world's total energy resources (see Chart 8.12).

But environmental problems reach far beyond our country, posing a global dilemma. Chart 8.13 describes the escalating destruction of the world's forest resources while Chart 8.14 lists the growing number of species whose future is endangered. Acid rain once fell only in rich western countries. Now, Asia is feeling its sting (see Chart 8.15). Almost everyone in the world will be adversely affected if average temperatures continue to rise. Chart 8.16 describes some factors contributing to global warming. The U.S. has done little to help solve this problem.

8.1 GDP is Misleading

The market knows the price of everything and the value of nothing. Economists like to measure our well-being by changes in the value of everything that is bought and sold divided by the population (the per-capita gross domestic product, or GDP). But this measure can be misleading. Sure, consumption increases. But traffic congestion, non-renewable energy use, and stress levels grow too. GDP calculations exclude these factors because they don't have obvious price tags.

When the Exxon Valdez spilled tons of crude oil into Alaskan waters, the money spent trying to clean up the mess actually increased GDP, while the long-term damage to the environment never found its way into the nation's economic ledgers.

The "Genuine Progress Indicator" (or GPI) provides an alternative measure for social well-being. It adds the value of non-market activities, such as household and volunteer work, and subtracts the costs of pollution, resource depletion, and less leisure time.

This indicator paints a very different picture of the amount of progress we've made in recent years. While per-capita GDP has nearly tripled between 1950 and 1997, the per-capita GPI has fallen since the late 1970s.

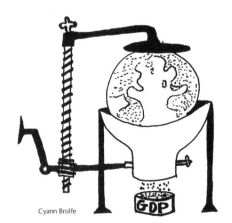

Cyann Brolfe

Gross Domestic Product and Genuine Progress Indicator, per capita, 1950-97 (in $1997)

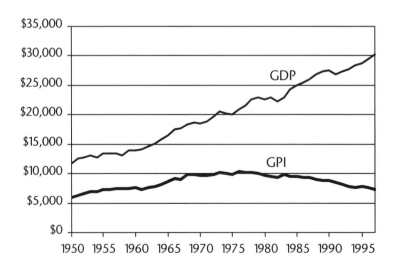

8.2 Gifts of Nature

People don't produce the most valuable services in the economy. Nature does. A recent study valued ecosystem services (such as soil formation, nutrient recycling, and climate regulation) at $33 billion, twice the value of the world's gross national product.

Putting a price on the environment may seem like a scary idea. But it underscores the need to consider the value of environmental services in economic policies. Making the economics of ecosystems more visible can help avoid bad decisions. For example, New York City recently discovered that it could save $6 to $8 billion by protecting its upstate watershed instead of building new water-treatment plants.

People put price tags on nature every day when they choose to develop a wetlands area or dam a river. They assume that the benefits automatically outweigh the costs. Without developing new ways of accounting for the real costs of human activities, we might not discover the true story until it's too late.

Total value of global goods and services in 1997 (in trillions of $US)

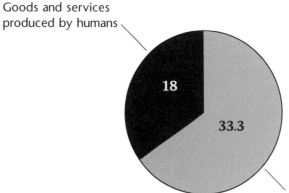

Goods and services produced by humans

18

33.3

Goods and services produced by nature (not including humans)

8.3 Toxic Polluters

Hold your nose. Toxic waste consists largely of chemicals such as ammonia, methanol and toluene that are released into the air or water or "injected" underground. Chemical colossus DuPont topped the list of the biggest toxic waste polluters in the United States in 1995. Recent data from the Environmental Protection Agency's toxic release inventory shows that the company released 85.8 million pounds. Other chemical and manufacturing firms were not far behind.

Overall, the U.S. chemical industry was responsible for more than 23,000 accidents involving toxic chemicals from 1993 to 1995. Political action committees linked to the Chemical Manufacturers' Association have donated millions to congressional campaigns. One of their primary goals is to weaken public regulation of the industry.

The top five toxic polluters in the U.S. in 1995

Company	Releases (millions of lbs.)	Lobbying ($millions spent)
DuPont	85.8	$1.7
Renco Group Inc.	73.5	—
ASARCO	65.0	$2.0
General Motors	38.9	$9.3
Monsanto	37.0	$4.0

8.4 Taking Out the Trash

Americans toss out mountains of garbage—in 1996, over 200 million tons of it. While we recycle more than ever before, the trash heaps continue to grow. In 1996, the non-recycled portion of solid waste per person was larger than the total amount of garbage in 1960.

Communities are trying to solve this problem. Many now require households and business to recycle. But industrial demand for recycled materials often doesn't keep up with supply. Other communities have started charging by the bag of trash. If disposal becomes too costly, some people resort to illegal dumping, which creates yet another set of environmental problems.

Environmentalists often advocate a broader set of policies that would include requirements for producers to use more recycled materials and less wasteful packaging.

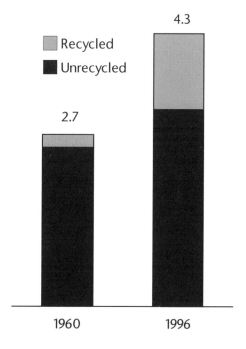

Pounds of solid waste per person in the U.S., per day

Recycled

Unrecycled

2.7

4.3

1960

1996

8.5 Environmental Racism

People of color are more likely than whites to live in communities with air pollution, toxic waste, and other environmental hazards.

- A recent study found that in neighborhoods targeted for expansion by toxic waste facilities, 25% of the population were people of color, compared to 18% in other areas.

- Communities of color often bear a disproportionate burden of the costs of industrial development. In Louisiana, 84% of the residents of the community nicknamed "cancer alley" are African-American. When yet another chemical company, producing polyvinyl chloride, chose to locate there, public pressures forced it to reconsider.

- The environmental movement has not traditionally focused its attention on communities of color. Recently, these communities themselves have started organizing. For example, in 1996, members of the Chippewa tribe blocked a mining company from dumping millions of gallons of sulfuric acid into an old copper mine to extract the last remaining bits of ore.

8.6 Hazardous Wastes

They're known as Superfund sites—places where highly toxic wastes have been recklessly dumped. In 1980, Congress created the Superfund to clean up areas with the worst problems. However, little progress has been made. More than 1,200 sites remain on the National Priority List and 73 million Americans live within 4 miles of at least one of them.

When costs of proper disposal run high, dumping waste becomes more attractive. And the private sector isn't the only one soiling the nest. At the nuclear weapons facility on Hanford Military Reservation in Washington, the government discharged over 400 billion gallons of radioactive water and liquid wastes into the ground.

The most toxic industries in the U.S. are chemical manufacturing, paper products, and primary metals. As the U.S. economy shifts away from these industries towards services, toxic releases will likely decline. However, as production shifts to developing countries, environmental problems could move overseas. Already the world produces 386 million tons of toxic waste each year, with an increasing share coming from poorer nations.

Hazardous waste sites on the National Priority List in 1997

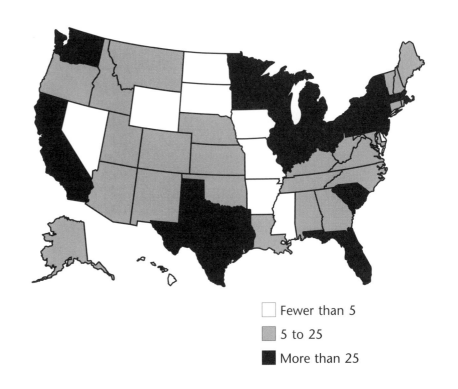

☐ Fewer than 5

▨ 5 to 25

■ More than 25

8.7 Septic Streams

Over one third of all our rivers and streams have bacterial counts in excess of government standards. Beginning in 1972, when national water-quality standards were first established, environmental policies helped to clean up America's waters. Fish returned to formerly polluted rivers and swimming holes became safe for people again. But in 1991, the trend reversed itself; today's waters are as polluted as they were two decades ago.

Untreated sewage and industrial effluents used to be the major sources of pollution. Now polluted runoff is becoming a serious problem; it's harder to track down and regulate because it comes from many different locations.

Freshwater ecosystems around the world are at risk, threatened by dams, chemical runoff, and acid rain. Already, freshwater habitats have lost a greater proportion of their species than the oceans or dry lands.

Percentage of rivers and streams with bacteria counts in violation of EPA standards, 1973-95

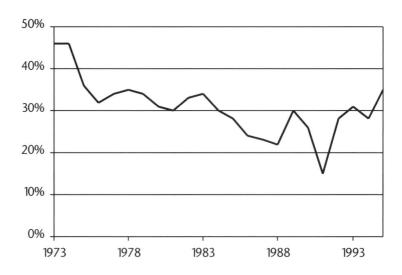

8.8 Environmental Industries

Conventional wisdom claims that you can't have your cake and eat it too; an economy can protect the environment or create jobs, but it can't do both. Employment numbers for environmental industries paint a different picture. Between 1980 and 1997, the number of jobs in environmental industries nearly tripled.

These numbers don't include the large number of jobs that recreation and tourism support. Maintaining the nation's parks and protected wildernesses creates a lot of jobs.

Instead of seeing the world as a set of fixed tradeoffs, sustainable approaches to development encourage raising standards of living while protecting the environment and improving people's quality of life.

Industrialized countries still have a long way to go on the path to sustainability. A recent study estimates that every person in affluent countries, like the U.S., Germany, or Japan, consumes an average of 50 to 94 tons of material resources each year. Producing food to feed one U.S. citizen causes 15 tons of soil erosion, while producing energy for each German citizen requires 32 tons of coal.

As global growth continues, gobbling up the material world is bad for the long-term health of the planet. A more balanced diet requires human activities to be both economically and environmentally sustainable.

Knickerbocker

Environmental industry employment (in thousands)

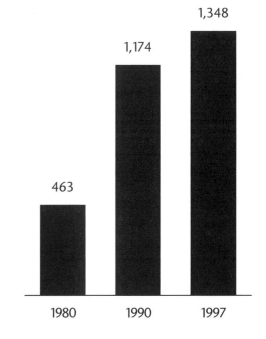

1980	1990	1997
463	1,174	1,348

8.9 The EPA Is Weak

The Environmental Protection Agency (EPA) could use some protection itself. Under-staffed and under-funded, the EPA has difficulties enforcing existing environmental regulations, let alone keeping abreast of new developments. In 1980, the EPA's total budget amounted to just 0.9% of all Federal spending, dropping to a dismal 0.4% by 1998. Despite the recent surplus of federal funds, the EPA budget has remained virtually constant as a fraction of total outlays throughout the 1990s.

The country's environmental regulations make up a complicated patchwork vulnerable to political manipulation. Congress often implements policies designed to please particular constituencies. The EPA could function better if comprehensive legislation allowed it to set priorities for dealing with the most serious problems first.

Environmental Protection Agency budget as a percentage of total federal budget

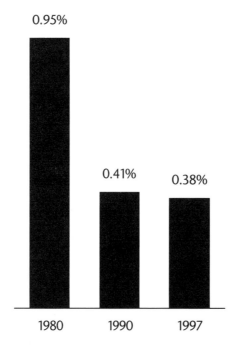

0.95%	0.41%	0.38%
1980	1990	1997

r. jay magill

8.10 Free-Market Environmentalism

The market frequently turns a blind eye to environmental destruction. However, the government doesn't always do a good job either. Subsidies to farmers, ranchers, and timber producers often worsen environmental problems. Sometimes a combination of markets and regulation works best.

- Some environmentalists advocate letting companies buy and sell "pollution permits" as a low-cost means of protecting the environment, rather than setting uniform regulations.

- The Clean Air Act Amendments of 1990 allowed the use of tradable pollution permits to reduce sulfur dioxide emissions and curb the threat of acid rain. Total emissions declined substantially as a result.

- Tradable permits could provide a means of efficiently tackling international environmental problems like the production of greenhouse gasses.

- Permit schemes cannot work, however, unless governments effectively monitor polluters and enforce the rules.

8.11 On the Road Again

At a time when a gallon of gas is cheaper than a gallon of bottled water, America's consumption of cars, trucks, and petroleum is the highest in the world. High incomes, limited public transportation, and a disregard for global environmental problems fuel this country's love affair with the road. The U.S. has 75 cars for every 100 adults and children; Europe has only 49 and Africa 2.2.

In every year since 1970, about 16 million additional cars traveled the world's roads. Industrialized countries account for most of this growth in consumption. The richest fifth of the world's countries consume 87% of all motor vehicles, the poorest fifth only 1%. The environmental impact is significant. Each year, cars account for 15% of all carbon dioxide emissions from fossil fuels.

New automotive technologies that use a cleaner source of power could help. But with the world's biggest consumer failing to pay the real costs of burning gasoline, few sustainable alternatives are economically feasible.

Number of registered motor vehicles for every 100 people in 1997

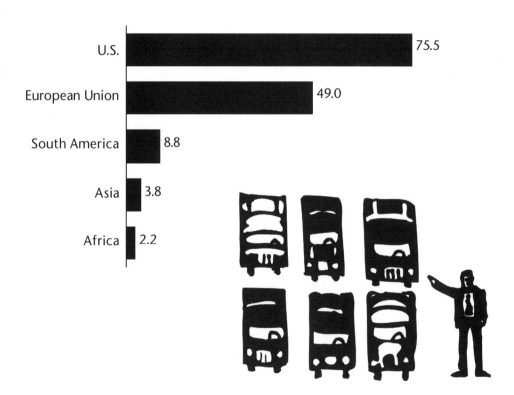

U.S.	75.5
European Union	49.0
South America	8.8
Asia	3.8
Africa	2.2

8.12 Energy Hogs

Why can't many developing countries keep up with the U.S. economy? Perhaps they just don't have the energy. American citizens consume, on average, an equivalent of 25,117 pounds of coal a year, compared to a world average of 4,395. Unequal energy consumption has important environmental implications. A child born in an industrialized nation contributes more to pollution over his or her life than do 30 to 50 children born in the developing world.

In 1995, coal, oil, gas, and nuclear power accounted for 80% of world electricity production. The use of non-renewable fossil fuels increases gas emissions which cause acid rain and contribute to global warming. Nuclear power produces waste materials which present an on-going environmental risk.

As developing countries continue to industrialize, the demand for energy around the world will continue to climb. This trend points to the urgent need to coordinate international efforts to balance energy consumption, economic development, and environmental sustainability.

THE U.S., WITH 5% OF THE WORLD'S *POPULATION,* USES 25% OF THE WORLD'S *ENERGY* AND EMITS 22% OF *ALL* CO_2 *PRODUCED...*

WELL--WE'RE *AMERICANS!* PROFLIGATE CONSUMPTION OF THE PLANET'S NATURAL RESOURCES IS OUR *BIRTHRIGHT!*

SUPPORT THE TROOPS

Tom Tomorrow

Per-capita energy consumption in pounds of coal equivalent in 1994

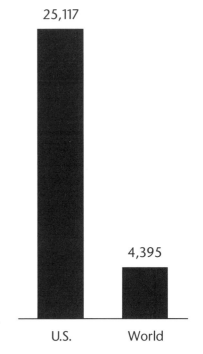

25,117

4,395

U.S.   World

8.13 When a Tree Falls...

Trees are crucial to the global ecosystem, providing precious habitat and stabilizing both climate and soil. But trees compete with other more immediately productive uses of land, such as grazing and growing food crops.

- The loss of forests in developing economies between 1990 and 1995 was 5,544,314 acres per year. While this rate is slightly smaller than the 6,272,764 acres lost each year between 1980 and 1990, many of the world's forests remain at risk.

- In the Brazilian Amazon, the annual deforestation rate declined from a peak of 4,942,089 acres in 1988 to 2,718,149 acres in 1991. However, by 1996 the rate had rebounded to an annual loss of 4,472,590 acres each year.

- In 1997, human activity and drought produced fires which destroyed between 150,000 and 300,000 acres of forest in Indonesia.

- Poverty, joblessness, and inequitable land distribution contribute to increased forest clearance for subsistence farming.

8.14 Endangered Species

Nearly 1,300 species of plants and animals around the world face a direct threat of extinction. Apart from the moral issues involved, we may lose species of great potential benefit by failing to take action.

The desire to make a quick buck is a big part of the problem. From orchids to rhino horns, the trade in rare plants and animals amounts to $17.5 billion each year. The World Wildlife Foundation estimates that one quarter of this trade is illegal. Efforts at protection were set back in 1997, when the Convention on International Trade in Endangered Species approved the sale of 60 tons of stockpiled elephant ivory.

Destruction of habitats also threatens plants and animals. In many parts of the world, poverty pushes people to intrude on fragile habitats. In other cases, careless development permanently disrupts ecosystems. Of course, some species thrive in urban concrete jungles: pigeons, rats, and cockroaches.

Matt Wuerker

Number of endangered species worldwide in 1998

Mammals	310
Birds	253
Reptiles	80
Amphibians	17
Fishes	78
Plants	554

8.15 Acid Rain Goes East

They called it a miracle. In the 1980s and 1990s, many economies in Asia grew at the fastest rates in the world. But the development of the Asian economies looks less miraculous if you subtract the costs of the rapid rise in air pollution. By 2000, emissions of sulfur dioxide (SO_2) in Asia will exceed those of North America and Europe combined.

Fossil fuels produce about 80% of the energy in Asia, with half of this amount coming from coal. Already the concentration of pollutants in the air of many Asian cities has reached dangerously high levels.

Rapid growth in emissions propels a dramatic increase in acid rain. Many ecosystems cannot accommodate high levels of acidity without suffering irreversible damage. Acid rain has already reduced agricultural and forestry production in China, India, and Korea. Such damage could be limited if countries used modern pollution control technologies, at an estimated cost of $90 billion each year.

Mean annual SO_2 emissions for selected cities in 1995 (micrograms/cubic meter)

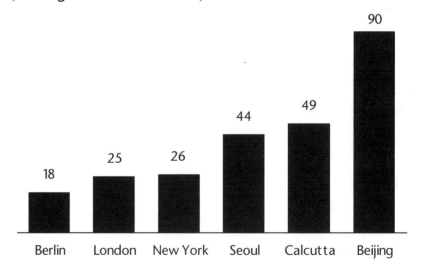

Berlin	London	New York	Seoul	Calcutta	Beijing
18	25	26	44	49	90

8.16 The Global Greenhouse

Things are heating up on spaceship earth. Most scientists agree that the planet has warmed almost one degree Fahrenheit over the past century. The extent to which this is due to human activities remains controversial, but evidence is growing that higher concentrations of certain gases in the atmosphere contribute to temperature hikes. We should be taking policy steps now to counter this trend.

Each year the U.S. releases more carbon dioxide (CO_2) than any other country. In 1995 alone, U.S. emissions totaled over 6 billion tons. Developing countries contribute far less to total greenhouse gases than do richer nations.

In 1997, a group of 167 nations signed the Kyoto Protocol, requiring high-emissions countries to reduce CO_2 output by 6% to 8%. The Protocol is an important step toward an international response to a global environmental problem. However, as of May 1999, the U.S. has failed to ratify it.

TOLES © 1998 The Buffalo News. Reprinted with permission of the UNIVERSAL PRESS SYNDICATE. All rights reserved.

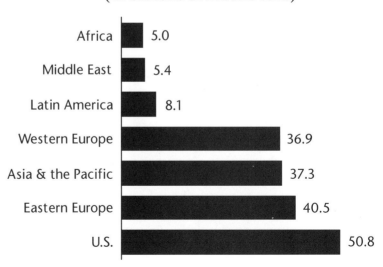

Cumulative CO_2 emissions, 1950-96 (in billions of metric tons)

Africa	5.0
Middle East	5.4
Latin America	8.1
Western Europe	36.9
Asia & the Pacific	37.3
Eastern Europe	40.5
U.S.	50.8

Chapter 9 **Macroeconomics**

Russell Christian

Macroeconomics ("macro" for short) focuses on factors that affect the growth of Gross Domestic Product (GDP), such as investment, profits, productivity, and interest rates. Powerful institutions, such as the Federal Reserve banking system, help steer the economy's course. That course is constantly changing in response to waves of technological change and tides of international trade. This chapter looks at where we have been and where we might be going.

Chart 9.1 documents a simple but important trend, a slowdown in the rate of growth of GDP since the 1970s. Increased political pressures are one result, since GDP defines the size of the economic pie. Chart 9.2 measures the slices currently received by workers and owners.

Long-run growth trends are overlaid by the ups and downs of the business cycle. Chart 9.3 maps the peaks and troughs of GDP growth over nearly five decades. During a recession, the value of output falls; during a recovery, it increases. Chart 9.4 describes some of the underlying forces driving this cycle.

Slow productivity growth helps explain slow GDP growth. Chart 9.5 illustrates a downward trend that has just begun to reverse itself, as investments in computer technology start paying off. Profit rates are a fundamental indicator of incentives to invest. Chart 9.6 points out that, after years of decline, profit rates are heading back up. This is good news for business, but won't help many workers unless the benefits begin to trickle down at a faster pace.

Despite improvements in the profit rate, many smaller businesses just can't get off the ground. Chart 9.7 shows that business failure rates have soared since the 1980s. While some businesses are going under, others are busy swallowing each other up. Chart 9.8 tracks the rapid increase in the value of mergers in recent years.

Why have new businesses been struggling so hard? High real interest rates—what people and firms have to pay to borrow money after taking inflation into account—provide one explanation. Chart 9.9 shows that real interest rates have been relatively high since the 1980s. What determines their levels? Federal Reserve Board policies exert a huge influence. Chart 9.10 explains how "the Fed" works.

Our entire banking system is undergoing rapid change. One major trend is consolidation, with small banks being incorporated into larger and larger ones, as shown in Chart 9.11. Other institutional developments are weakening the impact of financial regulation. As Chart 9.12 points out, more lending is taking place outside of the traditional banking system, free of the rules originally designed to guarantee stability.

How is the economy actually doing? Thumbs up if you base your assessment on the performance of the stock market in 1998 and early 1999. Chart 9.13 documents extraordinary growth in the Dow Jones average of stock prices. But the relationship between the Dow Jones and the economy's actual performance is complicated. If the economy is producing so much wealth for everyone, why is household borrowing at an all-time high? Chart 9.14 documents the steady growth in household debt. Today American families owe, on average, almost an entire year's income.

Investment in new productive resources is key to our economic future. But, as Chart 9.15 points out, investment in this country falls below that in other industrialized parts of the world. We like to buy what other people make, consuming far more of the world's output than we produce. The evidence? A growing trade deficit, which shows that our imports far exceed our exports (see Chart 9.16).

9.1 Slower Growth

Economic growth just isn't what it used to be. Looking back, the 1950s and 1960s were golden years in which average annual growth rates exceeded 4%. However, in the 1970s, the economy began to lose steam. In the 1990s, average growth slipped to 2.5% per year.

In the first years of both the 1980s and 1990s, the economy got a bad start. In fact, the recession in 1982 marked the worst slump since the Great Depression. However, after a short drop in 1991, the economy has enjoyed the longest period of uninterrupted expansion since the 1960s. Due to the growth slowdown, today's booms are more muffled than in the past. Many people don't sense much improvement from year to year.

Average annual growth rates, 1950-98

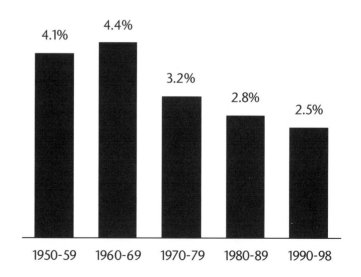

4.1%	4.4%	3.2%	2.8%	2.5%
1950-59	1960-69	1970-79	1980-89	1990-98

9.2 Dividing the Pie

The growth rate provides only one measure of economic prosperity. The distribution of total income fills out the picture by showing who benefits from growth. In 1997, the biggest share of national income went to pay employees, 72% of the total. Corporations received 12% of the total in profits.

The size of the slices has changed over time. In 1997, workers got a less-generous helping compared to the average for the 1970s and 1980s, while profits snatched up a larger share.

Today's economy embraces fewer small businesses but more big finance. In 1950, interest comprised about 1.2% of the total, growing to 6% by 1997. Over the same time period, proprietors' income was halved, from 16% in 1950 to 8% in 1997.

When thinking about the distribution of national income, keep in mind the number of people who share each slice. The biggest piece goes to workers, but this must be split up among the 130 million employees in the U.S. Far fewer people get any substantial part of the income from profits, interest, and rents.

Distribution of national income in 1997

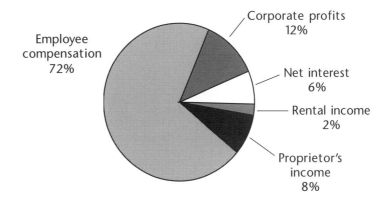

Employee compensation 72%

Corporate profits 12%

Net interest 6%

Rental income 2%

Proprietor's income 8%

r. jay magill

9.3 The Ups and Downs of GDP

We produce a lot of stuff in the U.S., over 8 trillion dollars worth annually. It's a lot more than we produced in 1950, but the increase hasn't been steady. Growth speeds up, then slows down, in a pattern known as the business cycle. Periods of expansion are followed by periods of recession (where the amount produced shrinks). Then the economy recovers and the cycle begins again.

During a slump, businesses have a hard time selling their products. They hire fewer workers, lay off some, and unemployment grows. Periods of recovery, on the other hand, can lead to inflation. Policy makers try to influence the business cycle by changing interest rates and the amount the government spends. However, their efforts don't always produce predictable results.

r. jay magill

**GDP growth rate, 1950-98
(grey bars indicate periods of recession)**

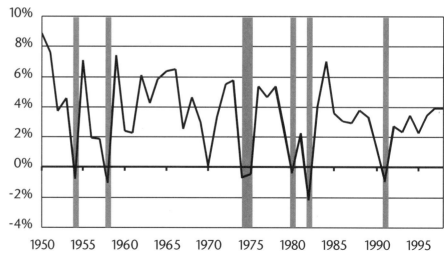

160

9.4 Business Cycles

An increase in real wages almost always threatens profits, and the relationship between wages, profits, and unemployment helps explain the business cycle. When profits are high, firms have an incentive to expand and hire more workers. But lower unemployment can eventually lead to higher wages and lower profits.

When profits fall, firms tend to lay off workers or to relocate to areas with lower wages. The resulting unemployment may then lower wages and restore profitability and economic growth. But if wages get too low, workers can't afford to buy what is produced. Unless demand is increased some other way, a recession can develop. Increased profits don't necessarily lead to increased economic growth within the U.S. because they may be invested overseas.

More surplus   Higher profits

Wages fall

More workers hired

Reserve pool of labor fills up

Labor pool drains

Wages go up

Automation, runaways, layoffs

Profits go down

Howard Saunders

9.5 Sagging Productivity

Getting the most out of the economy's resources propels growth forward. New technology, better equipment, more skills, and improved ways of organizing production all help to increase labor productivity, the value of what gets produced for each hour worked.

Average gains in U.S. labor productivity have been getting smaller and smaller. In the 1960s, productivity grew at nearly 3% per year but dropped to just over 1% in the 1990s.

If everyone gets a fair share, boosting productivity leads to better standards of living. However, over time, the growth of compensation has fallen behind productivity improvements. Workers have been getting a smaller and smaller fraction of the value of what they produce. Not letting workers share in the benefits could be one reason for slower productivity growth.

Growth of labor productivity and real compensation, 1960-98 (nonfarm business sector)

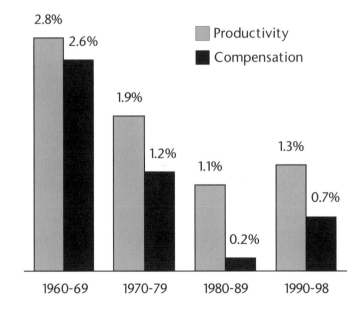

9.6 Profits in America

After drifting downward since the mid-1970s, the profit rate has begun to march back up. Have rates of return for investors finally found the high road to better performance? Or do recent improvements only amount to a temporary detour?

Oil shocks in the 1970s, high interest rates in the 1980s, low productivity growth, and growing global competition took their toll for two decades. Cheerleaders for the U.S. economy say higher profit rates show that America

has finally retooled and become globally competitive. But, such retooling can cause a lot of pain when workers face downsizing, belt-tightening, and lower real wages.

Profits of nonfinancial corporations as a percentage of nonfinancial corporate capital stock, 1950-97

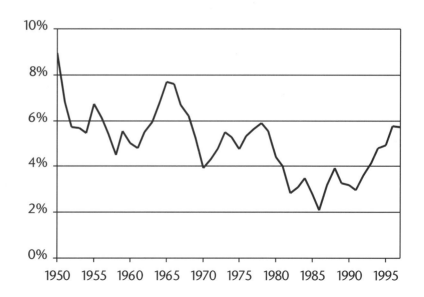

9.7 Business Failures

Have the pro-business policies of the past two decades delivered the goods? Not if you look at the trend in business failures. The mortality rate for firms increased sharply in the 1980s, reaching a post-Depression high in 1986. It has remained at high levels throughout the 1990s.

Failure is more common in some industries than in others. In 1997, services, retail trade, and construction accounted for over 65% of all failures. However, the textile industry had the highest rate, at 136 per 10,000 firms.

The blame lies largely with high interest rates. Big debt payments mop up cash flows and overwhelm small businesses. Even large firms that borrow a lot are susceptible. Intensified competition also puts pressures on businesses.

...the mystery of business failures.

Number of business failures, 1955-97

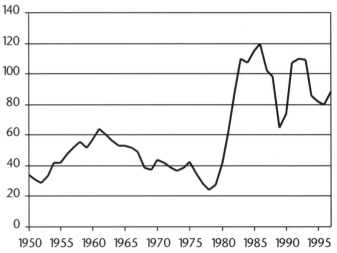

9.8 Merger Mania

It's a firm-eat-firm world out there. Instead of investing in new plants and expanding production, many businesses simply buy out the competition. In the U.S. the total value of mergers and acquisitions has skyrocketed, increasing from about $150 billion in 1985 to over $1 trillion by 1996.

In the 1980s, leveraged buyouts, in which borrowed money financed the takeovers, was a favorite method of merging. In the 1990s, rapid growth of stock prices created the financial muscle to pull firms together; leveraged buyouts became less important.

Businesses claim that mergers boost efficiency by eliminating duplication. The resulting job losses are certainly real, although evidence of productivity gains is hard to find.

Number of mergers, 1985-96
(transactions valued at $5 million or more)

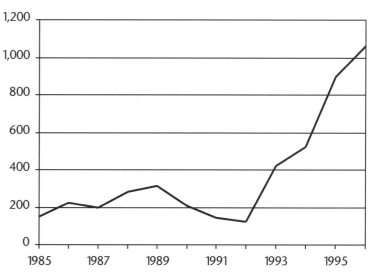

9.9 The Cost of Borrowing

We live in a world of high interest rates. Until the very end of the 1970s, average interest rates, adjusted for inflation, remained quite low. Since then, however, interest rates have risen and they continue to hover at historically high levels.

A number of factors contributed to the jump. In 1979, the Federal Reserve raised rates to combat inflation, resulting in one of the worst economic downturns in decades. Since that time, financial markets both at home and abroad have been deregulated. Fewer regulations give financiers an edge and allow them to demand higher returns.

High interest rates make it expensive to borrow. More costly credit can slow spending in important areas such as investment, dragging down economic growth and limiting the creation of good jobs.

Real yield on corporate Aaa bonds

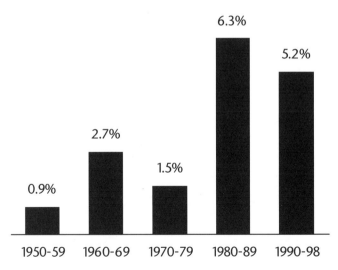

			6.3%	
				5.2%
	2.7%			
		1.5%		
0.9%				
1950-59	1960-69	1970-79	1980-89	1990-98

9.10 The Story Behind Interest Rates

Who determines interest rates?

The Fed, a.k.a. the Board of Governors of the Federal Reserve System, a group of bankers appointed by the president for 14-year terms, makes decisions that influence interest rates. Alan Greenspan has been the head of the Fed since 1987.

What does the Fed do?

It uses interest rates to steer the economy, raising them to induce recessions and lowering them to encourage economic growth. As the "bankers' bank," the Fed can change the rate of interest it charges its members and modify the supply of money in various ways.

What determines the Fed's decisions?

The Fed is supposed to buffer the business cycle and help the economy as a whole. But many critics argue that its policies benefit bankers and bond owners more than workers by keeping interest rates too high.

How does the Fed influence the stock market?

If the Fed gets worried about inflation, it raises interest rates. Stock prices may take a temporary dive, but the resulting economic slowdown puts a lid on wages and prices and helps restore long-run profitability. Unfortunately, it also increases unemployment.

9.11 Disappearing Banks

Ever get the feeling that a lot of banks in your community have recently changed names or been swallowed up by bigger banks? No, you aren't paranoid. Since 1984, small banks have been disappearing at an alarming rate.

Access to services has not declined. Many of the remaining banks have increased the number of branches they operate. As banking become more concentrated, competitive pressure gets weaker. Banks find it easier to invent new fees or increase old ones without worrying about losing customers.

Huge corporate mergers in the financial sector, such as the $73 billion deal between Citicorp and Travelers in 1998, accelerate this concentration of economic clout.

r. jay magill

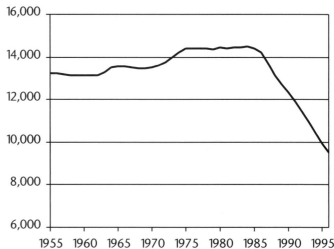

Number of banks in the U.S., 1955-96

9.12 The Changing Face of Finance

Where do loans come from? Most people assume that banks collect a community's savings and then use the deposits to lend money. But this Main Street U.S.A. version of finance is fast becoming history.

In the 1960s, savings and loans, credit unions, and commercial banks ac-counted for over 60% of net lending. In the 1990s, only 14% of lending could be attributed to these sources. Credit increasingly comes from non-bank sources, including investment companies, mutual funds, and specialty finance operations.

Less lending from more highly regulated institutions leads to greater instability in the financial system. Deregulation triggered the savings and loan crisis of the 1980s, and financiers are still inventing new ways to dodge the remaining government controls.

Bank lending as a percentage of financial sector lending, 1950-97

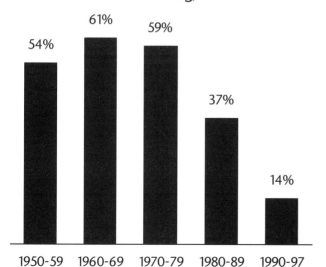

169

9.13 Keeping Up With the Dow Jones

For many investors, the U.S. stock market has been a stairway to heaven. Despite occasional jitters, stock prices have climbed continually since the early 1980s, making some people incredibly rich. The Wall Street faithful have their eyes set on still greater heights, but skeptics wonder when they'll plunge back to earth.

The majority of people, who own few if any shares, haven't been able to keep up with the boom. Between 1975 and 1998, stock prices increased 975%, but real wages fell. The Dow Jones keeps setting new records; in the first half of 1999, it broke the 10,000-point barrier.

The stock market does have an impact on the real economy. Wealthier households have gone on a spending spree in recent years, increasing total demand for certain goods and services. But what will happen if this demand crashes, along with stock prices, as happened in 1929?

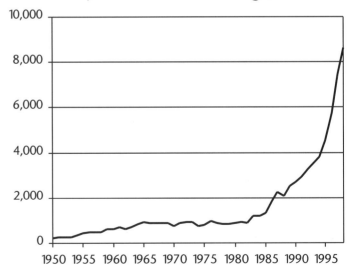

Dow Jones Industrial Average, 1950-98

9.14 Debt Trap

If slow-growing wages have got you down, maybe your junk mail can cheer you up. Credit card companies are always looking for new customers.

In 1950, the total debt of households amounted to about 35% of disposable income. By 1997, it had risen to nearly 100%.

For many over-indebted Americans, losing a job can mean losing a car or a home. High interest rates increase the pressure. Large payments on outstanding debt squeeze household resources.

Some families just can't cope. Personal bankruptcies have doubled in the past decade; a record 1.3 million people filed in 1997.

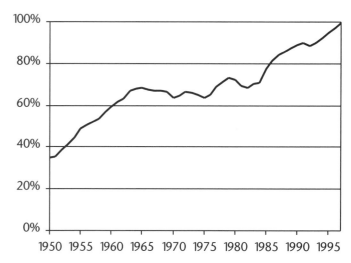

Household debt as a percentage of after-tax income, 1950-97

9.15 Investing for the Future

Investment today determines our standard of living tomorrow. Money devoted to developing new technologies and improving our capital stock pays off in the long run. But even though the U.S. economy is booming, our investment rates are relatively low.

In 1997, 19% of our Gross Domestic Product (GDP) went toward investment, compared to 20% in the European Union, 24% in Australia, and 30% in Japan (gross investment is a measure that doesn't take into account the depreciation of the existing capital stock).

U.S. investors like to move their money around, seeking short-term gains. Perhaps they are afraid of tying up financial resources in long-term investments. The temptation to make a quick buck can prove expensive in the long run, particularly for those who depend on the ability of the U.S. economy to generate gains in productivity and wages.

Gross investment as a percentage of GDP in 1997

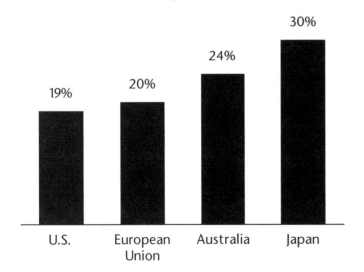

Nick Thorkelson

172

9.16 Unbalanced Trade

America is import-crazy. For decades, the importance of trade in the economy has risen. However, in every year since 1975, the U.S. has run a trade deficit, importing more from other countries than we export.

More than half of our imports come from other industrialized countries. However, the biggest share of the deficit can be traced to trade with developing economies. American businesses and consumers benefit from low wages and cheap production, but many of these countries are so poor they cannot turn around and buy U.S. exports.

Does a trade deficit really matter? Think of it this way: By consuming more of the world's goods and services than we make, we are living on borrowed production. What will happen when our debts come due?

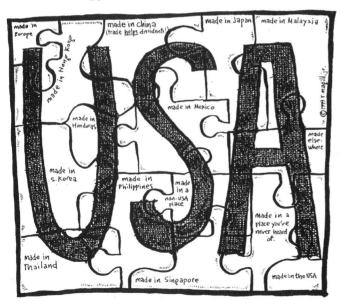

Imports, exports, and the balance of trade, 1950-97

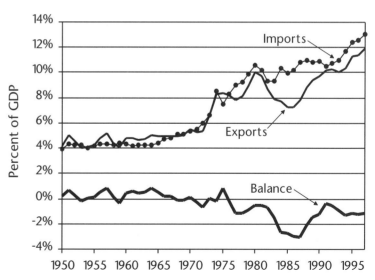

Chapter 10 The Global Economy

Russell Christian

A trip through today's global marketplace usually means a walk on the wild side. No one knows what lies around the next corner. Financial crises wreak havoc in some countries while stock markets create paper billionaires in others. Don't blink. You might miss something. In the time it takes to grab a drive-through burger, billions of dollars have zipped from one corner of the world to another.

It's a high-stakes game in which many countries try to please investors rather than meet the needs of their citizens. This chapter looks at important developments in the international marketplace, including trends in trade, finance, and basic human needs.

Chart 10.1 shows that the engine of the global economy actually slowed in the 1990s, as compared to the 1980s. Unemployment has become a more serious problem in many countries in the world than in the United States, which has successfully ridden a boom (see Chart 10.2).

Charts 10.3 and 10.4 look at international flows of capital. Firms expand abroad in search of cheaper wages, lower taxes, less regulation, and bigger markets. In recent years, U.S. companies have been acquiring larger numbers of foreign firms. A substantial fraction of the profits U.S. businesses earn comes from overseas.

Once upon a time, most developing countries specialized in agricultural exports such as bananas and coffee. Times have changed, and manufacturing has spread. Chart 10.5 points out that manufactured goods now account for about the same fraction of exports in developing and industrialized economies. But low-wage competitors don't always have the edge. The U.S. still imports most of its goods from high-wage, developed countries such as the European Community (Chart 10.6).

Most developing countries are trying to increase their exports, a process which often increases women's participation in paid employment. More jobs mean new opportunities, but women often provide a pool of cheap labor without enough bargaining power to capture much of the economic gain (see Chart 10.7). Many countries set up Export Processing Zones (EPZs) with low taxes and relaxed regulations to entice prospective investors, with mixed results for workers (see Chart 10.8).

Foreign Direct Investment, or FDI, can provide funds to finance job-creating productive activities. But as Chart 10.9 indicates, most FDI goes to rich, industrialized countries. Chart 10.10 shows that poorer countries are likely to attract more short-term than long-term commitments. The rapid movement of short-term funds can trigger devastating financial crises. International transactions have mushroomed in the United States, as well as in developing countries (see Chart 10.11). European countries are now moving to a common currency, the Euro, which will increase their influence in financial markets (see Chart 10.12).

Your country—love it or leave it. As leaving becomes easier, government regulations and restrictions are becoming increasingly passé. Chart 10.13 documents the liberalization of trade and removal of regulations around the world. Large-scale financial crises are one result. Chart 10.14 summarizes some of the worst disasters in recent years.

If international financial problems were simply a question of wealthy investors losing their shirts, we wouldn't all need to worry. But as Chart 10.15 shows, the reality is sadly different. A fall in the value of a country's currency can be extraordinarily disruptive. Sudden increases in food and fuel prices make basic necessities less affordable.

Global inequalities remain extreme. As Chart 10.16 indicates, hunger remains a devastating problem in many regions. Differences between rich and poor countries are as extreme as those between eighteenth-century lords of the manor and their peasant serfs (see Chart 10.17). Simply increasing growth rates of GDP will not help. Chart 10.18 points out that some relatively rich countries actually have higher infant-mortality rates than much poorer, but more egalitarian, regimes. The benefits of growth should be more widely distributed.

10.1 Global Slowdown

The wheels of international growth aren't spinning as fast as they used to. In the 1980s, world Gross Domestic Product (GDP) grew at over 3% per year; between 1990 and 1996, the average slipped to only 2.2%.

Growth in the large industrialized countries has slowed down, reducing the world average. The economies in much of sub-Saharan Africa and Eastern Europe have also lagged behind in recent years. On the other hand, Latin America, the Middle East, and North Africa looked better in the 1990s.

The stars of the past two decades were the East Asian countries, boasting breakneck annual growth rates of 10% between 1990 and 1996. Then they hit a brick wall. Devastating financial crises in 1997-98 pushed most of the region into recession.

Many economists argue that less regulated and more closely connected economies will grow much faster. But global growth hasn't increased, despite the removal of regulations and barriers in many countries throughout the world.

Average growth rate of world GDP

1980-90	3.1%
1990-96	2.2%

r. jay magill

10.2 Unemployment Elsewhere

Need a job? Join the club. High unemployment continues to plague countries around the world, including those with well-developed economies.

A temporary economic slump can't explain these high jobless rates. Many European countries have been battling double-digit unemployment for years. Before the 1980s, unemployment in much of Europe was on a par with other industrialized regions. Since then, high interest rates and slow growth have taken their toll; as firms feel the squeeze, policies protecting the welfare of workers have come under attack.

Unemployment in the U.S. is much lower. But don't be fooled. In part, this reflects more unskilled, part-time jobs (and higher incarceration rates). Recently, both Germany and the U.S. have been creating new well-paid and secure jobs at about the same rate—2.6% each year.

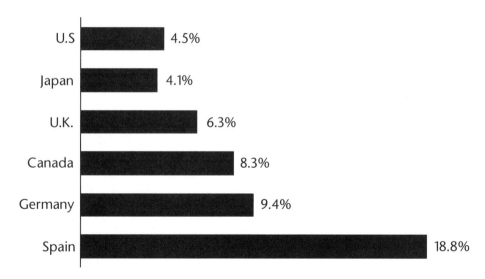

Standardized unemployment rates of selected industrialized countries in 1998

U.S	4.5%
Japan	4.1%
U.K.	6.3%
Canada	8.3%
Germany	9.4%
Spain	18.8%

10.3 Cross-Border Conglomerates

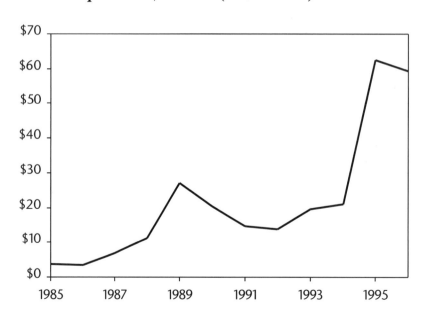

When it comes to national borders, ownership knows no bounds. In recent years, corporations have been orchestrating an unprecedented volume of international mergers. The value of overseas acquisitions by U.S. firms has grown from $3.7 billion in 1985 to nearly $60 billion in 1996.

International markets are becoming more connected, creating an incentive for more cross-border acquisitions, as the recent mergers of Daimler/Chrysler and Ford/Volvo demonstrate. Grabbing a bigger chunk of the global market gives firms opportunities for more control and greater profits.

As corporations continue to expand their operations across national boundaries, monitoring and regulating their behavior becomes more difficult. Giant global businesses can use their new-found flexibility to move operations from place to place and take advantage of lower taxes and looser regulations.

Value of U.S. overseas acquisitions, 1985-96 (in $billions)

10.4 Have Profits, Will Travel

U.S. corporations have been on a voyage of discovery, scouting the earth in search of profit opportunities. They've been quite successful. In 1950, foreign profit made up only 3% of all before-tax profits. In 1997, 13% came from overseas.

Maintaining international operations helps businesses stay competitive. But they also become more footloose. Plans to downsize at home and move abroad put American communities at risk of losing jobs.

Companies can use their cross-border status to reduce taxes and dodge regulations. For example, manipulating the prices one division charges another allows multinationals to lower their reported profits and to avoid high tax rates. Maintaining public infrastructure and education becomes tougher when governments have less money to spend.

Foreign profits of U.S. firms as a percentage of all before-tax profits, 1950-97

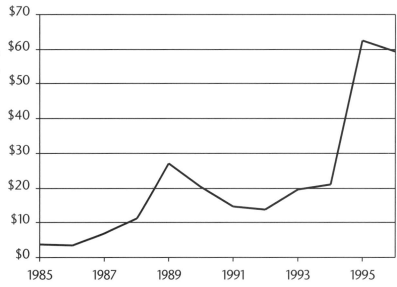

10.5 Trade Transformation

The banana republics of the past are fast becoming the manufacturers of the future. For years, developing countries depended on exporting raw materials and unprocessed commodities to rich countries. Today, manufactured goods from many of these countries are actively competing with the industrialized world.

In 1985, manufactured goods only accounted for 29% of the total exports from developing countries. By 1996, manufacturing was 77% of the total, nearing the same proportion as in industrialized countries.

Rapid growth in manufacturing from developing nations unleashes more competition in world markets. Benefits can be few and far between. Such competition often creates pressures to keep wages low, to limit protection for workers, and to avoid environmental regulations. Countries end up running a "race to the bottom" in which many of the gains from export growth simply vanish.

R.J. Magill

Manufacturing exports as a percentage of total exports, 1985-96

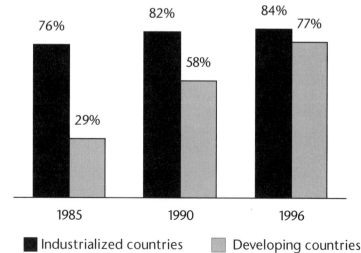

■ Industrialized countries ▨ Developing countries

10.6 Cheap Labor and Imports

Do low-wage countries gobble up American jobs, feeding off this country's willingness to buy cheap imports? While this story might play well during election campaigns, the reality is much more complex.

Some firms do travel the globe, looking for rock-bottom labor costs. But the U.S. currently imports more from high-wage trading partners like Canada, the European Union, and Japan than it does from low-wage competitors. In fact, the average hourly compensation in the top 28 importing countries was $15.25, not much lower than in the U.S.

High levels of education, good public infrastructure, and productivity improvements can be more important than wages. If developing countries were able to provide these amenities, they would make great inroads.

Hourly labor costs in U.S. and major trading partners in 1997

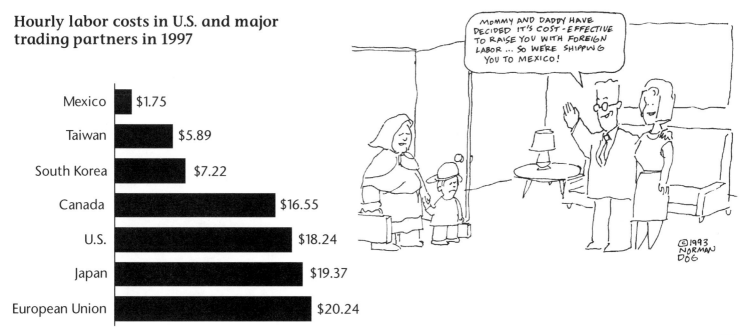

Mexico	$1.75
Taiwan	$5.89
South Korea	$7.22
Canada	$16.55
U.S.	$18.24
Japan	$19.37
European Union	$20.24

© 1993 NORMAN DOG

10.7 Trade, Women, and Work

The countries that have been most successful at increasing their exports all rely on a similar strategy: moving more women into paid employment. Export-oriented industries often employ young women who lack other opportunities and seldom plan to remain after marriage. Such workers are difficult to unionize and have little bargaining power.

The strong relationship between changes in women's paid employment and changes in the importance of trade also reflects the policies of international agencies such as the World Bank and the International Monetary Fund, which have compelled many countries to adopt policies aimed at moderating wages and cutting government spending. Squeezes on household resources tend to push young women into the labor force.

Trade-related employment can benefit women by providing new economic opportunities outside the home. But the benefits are limited when job tenure is short and pay is low.

Male workers employed outside the export sector tend to earn much higher wages.

Women's paid employment rates and trade, 1970-94

y-axis: Change in trade as a % of GDP
x-axis: Change in women's paid employment

Tom Tomorrow

10.8 Export Processing Zones

You are traveling through an economic dimension, in which tax laws and regulations have no meaning. You have just entered an export processing zone.

Export processing zones (EPZs) provide benefits to firms to encourage trade-related growth and job creation. The packages often include tax breaks, no tariffs on imported materials, and relaxed regulations. In turn, companies in EPZs commit to manufacturing goods for export.

While some EPZs just offer business giveaways, others aim to keep wages low and hours long. Workers seldom develop transferable skills on the job. In many cases, efforts to organize a union to improve conditions are met with fierce resistance.

Export processing zones, by region in 1996

Latin America & the Caribbean	232
Asia & the Pacific	227
Africa	47
Middle East	39

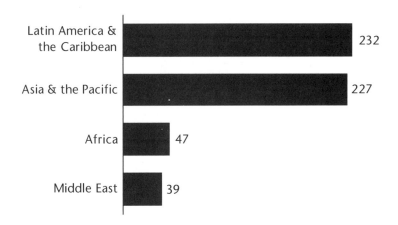

IMPROVE YOUR BOTTOM LINE WITH DISPOSABLE WORKERS

THEY SLICE, THEY DICE —THEY'LL DO ANYTHING *

Save millions with the Part-Time and Temp Models. No Vacations! No Benefits! Noooo PENSIONS!!

Save even more with our "Off-Shore Models" free of any safety or environmental regulations! Chinese Prisoners, South American Girls

GET 'EM WHEN THEY'RE YOUNG USE 'EM—ABUSE 'EM—AND THEN TOSS 'EM! THEY'RE DISPOSABLE!

* THEY DON'T HAVE A UNION!

M WUERKER

10.9 Foreign Direct Investment

Knickerbocker

They say nature abhors a vacuum. If this were true for the world economy, investment would flow quickly from industrialized countries to poorer nations. Just the opposite happens: richer countries attract most of the international investment.

Cross-border investment falls into several categories. To qualify as foreign direct investment, or FDI, a company must own at least 10% of the value of a business. Unlike more short-term flows of capital, FDI usually comes with a willingness to set up shop in another country. For developing countries, it can mean more stable sources of finance and less borrowing.

Industrialized countries attract nearly 70% of all FDI because of high-income consumers, well-educated workers, and extensive infrastructure. Developing countries compete for FDI by cutting government spending and promising lower wages, strategies which undermine the benefits FDI is supposed to deliver.

Distribution of foreign direct investment in 1997

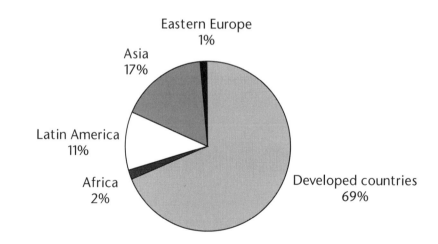

Eastern Europe 1%

Asia 17%

Latin America 11%

Africa 2%

Developed countries 69%

10.10 Fair-Weather Finance

"Here today, gone tomorrow" would make a good slogan for today's financial markets. As finance becomes more mobile, large numbers of investors can pack up their money and leave a country overnight. When financiers take flight, they often leave behind an economic mess, requiring billion-dollar rescue packages to straighten things out.

Low- and middle-income countries find themselves at greater risk as the type of investment they attract shifts. Portfolio investment describes short-term investment in stocks and bonds. In contrast, foreign direct investment usually comes with a more long-term commitment. Between 1990 and 1996, portfolio investment in low- and middle-income countries increased over six times faster than foreign direct investment.

Without more attention directed at monitoring and controlling short-term flows, the risks of future financial crises remain high.

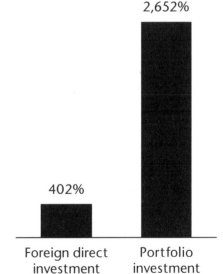

Increases in international financial flows to low- and middle-income countries (1990-96)

2,652%

402%

Foreign direct investment

Portfolio investment

WITH THE GLOBAL ECONOMY AT A STANDSTILL, FINANCIAL MARKETS COLLAPSED. HUNDREDS OF MILLIONS OF STARVING PEOPLE BROUGHT DOWN EVERY SINGLE GOVERNMENT. A MOB IS DOWN IN THE LOBBY, DEMANDING YOUR HEAD ON A STICK.

BUT ALL THIS NEW GLOBAL ECONOMY-FREE TRADE STUFF WAS SUPPOSED TO BE FOR US!

WE'LL REVISIT IT AFTER YOUR FUNERAL, SIR.

Ted Rall

10.11 High-Speed Investment

If you think the Concorde can move across borders at lightning speeds, check out today's financial markets. More money whizzes around the world than ever before. U.S. cross-border transactions in stocks and bonds made up only 4% of GDP in 1975, but zoomed to 230% by 1998.

Growth in trade explains only a small part of the expansion in international transactions. When large sums of money change hands nowadays, people are usually buying and selling financial assets, rather than exchanging goods and services. High finance overshadows real production.

Large surges in cross-border finance weaken government ability to influence economic outcomes. Investors can simply hop from country to country, skipping those with policies they find distasteful.

U.S. cross-border transactions in bonds and equities (as a percentage of GDP)

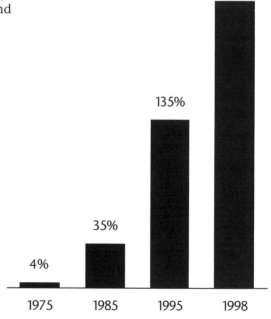

10.12 The Euro

In the 19th century, the British pound sterling ruled the world. For the next hundred years, the U.S. dollar took control. What currency will dominate the 21st century? The Euro is a major contender.

On January 1, 1999, 11 countries made world history when they merged their monetary systems and created the Euro. Their combined GDP falls slightly short of that of the U.S. However, more countries, such as Britain and Sweden, could join in the near future. If this happens, the Euro will become the currency of the single largest economic bloc in the world.

As the Euro gains prominence, monetary policies in Europe could have as big an impact as U.S. actions do today. While the final outcome is anyone's guess, the Euro could reshape the landscape of international finance for years to come.

OLIPHANT ©1997 UNIVERSAL PRESS SYNDICATE. Reprinted with permission. All rights reserved.

Gross Domestic Product of currency areas in 1997 (in millions of $US)

187

10.13 Global Free-For-All

In the world of international finance, countries have been opening the stable doors for years; now they wonder how so many horses got out. Adoption of policies that relax controls on finance have outpaced efforts to rein in unpredictable flows. These changes have increased cross-border transactions by leaps and bounds, resulting in greater instability.

Without control over the behavior of financial flows, governments often must bribe investors to stay. High interest rates provide one way of improving investment returns. Tax breaks and business subsidies are another. Recently, the number of such incentive programs has multiplied.

Spending more on tax breaks and subsidies means there's less to spend on education, health care, and public services. Social welfare is subordinated to the needs of financial markets.

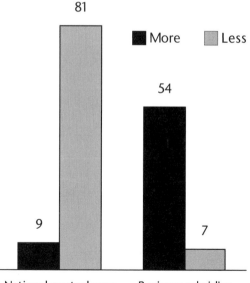

Worldwide changes in national regulations by type in 1997

10.14 International Meltdown

Greater capital mobility and less regulation have helped make the 1990s a decade of financial crises.

Mexico, 1995: When the Mexican government tried to gently lower the value of the peso, investors pulled out and the currency went into a free-fall. Consumer prices and interest rates shot up, squeezing family incomes. It took a $50 billion bail-out package to stabilize the situation.

East Asia, 1997-98: What began as a fall in the value of the Thai currency ended up pushing many regional economies into recession. Like a brush fire, the crisis spread to South Korea, Indonesia, Malaysia, and Japan. Banks failed, riots broke out, and the GDPs of the afflicted countries shrank.

Russia, 1998: In July, the International Monetary Fund arranged a $22 billion emergency loan to Russia. One month later the value of the ruble plunged, making consumer goods unaffordable and repayment of foreign loans nearly impossible. The U.S. stock market reacted with a sudden drop in prices.

Brazil, 1999: Despite a prearranged rescue package of $41 billion, the *real* lost much of its value. High interest rates and less spending could worsen economic conditions in Brazil.

TOLES © 1998 The Buffalo News. Reprinted with permission of the UNIVERSAL PRESS SYNDICATE. All rights reserved.

10.15 Devaluation Hits Home

What can topple governments, toss millions into poverty, and wipe out economic growth in a matter of days? An alien invasion? The Y2K bug? A more common occurrence is a rapid decline in value of a nation's currency.

If the value of a currency plunges, goods purchased from other countries become more expensive. Higher prices for food and other basic commodities cut into incomes, rapidly lowering standards of living. Speculative investments and the unregulated flow of finances have a destabilizing impact.

When the *rupiah*, Indonesia's currency, took a nosedive in mid-1997, consumer prices flew up. As many as 55 million people slipped into poverty, ethnic conflicts broke out, and President Suharto lost control of the government after 32 years in power.

yeah right!! like money problems all the way over there could affect us!!

r. jay magill

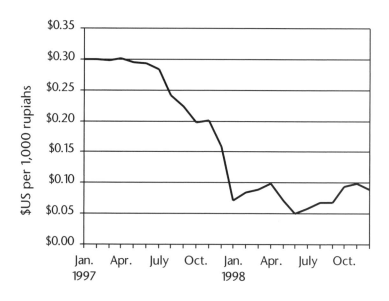

Exchange rate of the rupiah in Indonesia, January 1997-December 1998

190

10.16 Crying for Food

I n a world where many dinner parties carefully observe the aesthetic protocols of designer Martha Stewart, a vast number of children can't take a single meal for granted. In sub-Saharan Africa, nearly one third of children under five don't get enough to eat. In South Asia, over half are underweight.

Scarcity isn't the problem; poverty is. The world produces enough food for everyone, but the poorest just can't afford what they need. Falling currencies and raising prices have increased food costs in many countries.

In most developing countries, overall consumption of calories and protein has grown in recent decades. But consumption remains far below the level of developed countries. And deficiencies of certain key nutrients, such as Vitamin A, iron, and iodine, cause serious health problems.

Percentage of children under 5 who are underweight, 1990-97

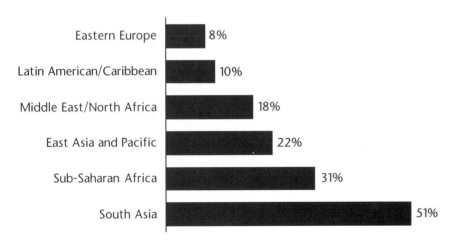

Region	Percentage
Eastern Europe	8%
Latin American/Caribbean	10%
Middle East/North Africa	18%
East Asia and Pacific	22%
Sub-Saharan Africa	31%
South Asia	51%

I mean, dear Lord — If they really cared about food, then how come they don't know how to make cashew-nutmeg drops OR lobster Mornay?!

©1999 magill, jr.

10.17 The Consumption Gap

The inequality within the global economy far surpasses that within any individual nation. The richest fifth of all countries enjoys 86% of worldwide consumption while the poorest fifth barely gets 1%.

In 1995, per-capita consumption expenditures averaged $15,910 in industrialized countries, but only $275 in South Asia and $340 in sub-Saharan Africa. Despite these vast inequalities, rich countries still want more. Studies of U.S. households indicate that the income people require to fulfill their consumption goals doubled between 1986 and 1994.

The world isn't getting any more equal. In most low income countries, spending on private consumption has declined by about 1% every year for the past 15 years, while the world average has grown by 3%.

World consumption expenditures in 1995

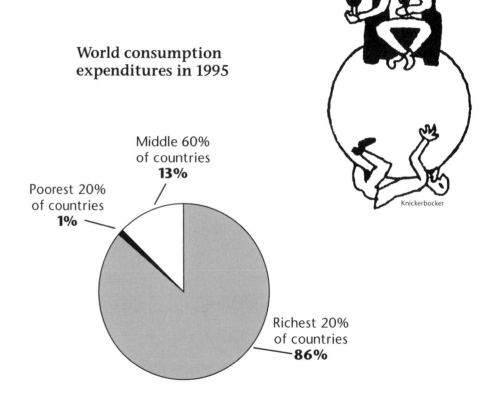

Middle 60% of countries **13%**

Poorest 20% of countries **1%**

Richest 20% of countries **86%**

Knickerbocker

10.18 Does Economic Growth Deliver the Goods?

When it comes to meeting basic needs, per-capita GDP just doesn't cut it. The distribution of income and the provision of public services is more important.

Armenia, with less than one-twelfth of the GDP per capita of Argentina, outranks that country on quality-of-life indicators such as infant mortality rates, secondary-school enrollment, and number of physicians per 1,000 people.

Brazil generates far more income per person than China but suffers from higher infant mortality rates.

South Africa and Croatia have similar levels of GDP per capita, but a more equal distribution of income helps Croatia outperform South Africa on most human-development indicators. Croatia's infant mortality is one-fifth that of South Africa and children have much better access to basic immunizations.

Russell Christian

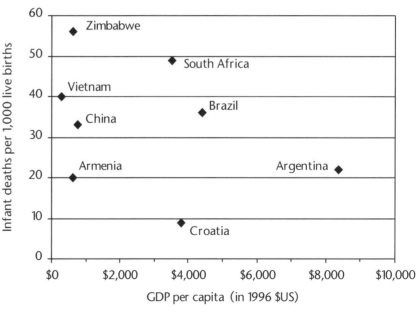

Infant mortality vs. GDP per capita in 1996

Toolkit

T.1 A Guide to General Sources

This section provides a guide to sources of data and analysis that are useful in economic research. It begins with an overview of general sources, then provides further information for each chapter topic. Use the detailed references in the Sources section of this book to track down or update specific facts and figures.

The Internet has made a wealth of economic information more accessible than ever. This section includes addresses for a number of the most useful sites for finding the type of economic information presented in the pages of this book. In many cases, statistics and entire publications will be available on-line. In other cases, the websites only provide ordering information. For more details (and useful links) check out this book's companion website at www.fguide.org.

- The two best sources of general economic data are the *Statistical Abstract of the U.S.* (www.census.gov/statab/www), published by the U.S. Bureau of the Census (www.census.gov), and *The Economic Report of the President* (www.access.gpo.gov/eop), published by the President's Council of Economic Advisors. Both can be downloaded from the Web. New editions normally become available in February from the Government Printing Office (www.access.gpo.gov). Catalogs of GPO publications are available from the Superintendent of Documents, Stop SM, Washington, DC 20402.

- FedStats (www.fedstats.gov) is an extremely useful website with links to a large number of federal agencies and departments. See also the Department of Commerce site called Stat-USA (www.stat-usa.gov).

- Short, interesting, and useful articles about current economic events are published monthly in *Dollars and Sense*, by the Economic Affairs Bureau, Inc., 1 Summer Street, Somerville, MA 02143. Tel: 617-628-8411 (www.dollarsandsense.org). More academic yet accessible articles are published bi-monthly in *Challenge*, 80 Business Park Drive, Armonk, NY 10504.

- The major publications of the business press, including *The Wall Street Journal, Fortune, Forbes,* and *Barron's,* are all useful, but *Business Week* usually offers the most systematic analysis of economic trends. For a distinctly anticorporate approach, see T*he Left Business Observer.* 250 West 85th Street, New York, NY 10024. Tel: 212-874-4020. (www.panix.com/~dhenwood/LBO_home.html).

- For more in-depth reading, *The State of Working America 1998-99* by the Economic Policy Institute (www.epinet.org) offers a comprehensive analysis of the way economic trends affect working Americans.

- The National Priorities Project provides helpful information and analysis on the government's budget priorities. 160 Main Street, Suite 6, Northampton, MA 01060. Tel:

413-584-9556. (www.natprior.org/home/index.html). United for a Fair Economy has developed a range of publications, educational materials, and workshops that focus on wealth and income distribution. 37 Temple Place, 2nd Floor, Boston, MA 02111. Tel: 617-423-2148 (www.stw.org).

- The Center for Popular Economics provides workshops on economic literacy, international economics, and urban economic issues. Contact us at P.O. Box 785, Amherst, MA 01004. Tel: 413-545-0743 (www.ctrpopec.org).

Chapter 1: Owners. Every October for the past several years, *Forbes* magazine has published a feature article describing the richest 400 people in the U.S. in that year. In late spring or early summer, *Fortune* ranks the top industrial corporations of the year and provides considerable information about their performance. In May, *Business Week* usually publishes a list of the highest-paid corporate executives.

For a critical analysis of the impact of money on electoral outcomes, contact the Center for Responsive Politics, 1320 19th St. NW, Suite 620, Washington DC, 20036. Tel: 202-857-0044 (www.opensecrets.org/home).

Chapter 2: Workers. Monthly issues of the Bureau of Labor Statistics' *Employment and Earnings* (*EE*) are the best source of up-to-date information on labor force participation, industry, occupation, earnings, and unemployment. The January issue provides annual averages for the preceding year. The bureau also publishes *Monthly Labor Review*, which often includes articles on special topics such as displaced workers. The website for the Bureau of Labor Statistics is www.stat.bls.gov. The American Federation of Labor (AFL-CIO) also maintains a useful website at www.aflcio.org/home.

In 1994 the BLS changed some of the definitions it used in its labor-force survey. As a result, some figures for 1994 and later years, such as the unemployment rate, are not perfectly comparable with those for earlier years. For more details see "Revisions in the Current Population Survey Effective Jan. 1994," *EE*, Feb. 1994.

Chapter 3: Women. The Bureau of the Census periodically publishes special reports on women. Another useful source of reports and analysis is the Institute for Women's Policy Research. 1400 20th St. NW, Suite 104, Washington, D.C. 20036. Tel: 202-785-5100 (www.iwpr.org). For international comparisons, see *The World's Women 1970-1990* and *The World's Women 1995*, published by the United Nations (www.un.org).

Chapter 4: People of Color. The Bureau of the Census (www.census.gov) publishes reports periodically with useful analysis and statistics. A great summary document is *Changing America: Indicators of Social and Economic Well-Being by Race and Hispanic Origin,* published by the Council of Economic Advisers for the President's Initiative on Race in 1998. (www.access.gpo.gov/eop/ca/index.html)

Chapter 5: Government Spending. Every January, the president proposes a budget for the next fiscal year to Congress, detailed in *The Budget of the U.S. Government* and summarized in *The Budget in Brief.* The best source for historical data on revenue and taxation is *The U.S. Budget, Historical Tables*. Look at the Office of Management and Budget website for easy access to many of these publications (www.whitehouse.gov/omb). These publications are also available from the Government Printing Office (see introduction to this section).

The Center on Budget and Policy Priorities, 777 Capital Street NE, Suite 705, Washington, DC 20002, Tel: 202-408-1080 (www.cbpp.org), publishes regular reports on government spending, particularly as it affects low-income Americans. Citizens for Tax Justice, 1311 L Street NW, Washington, DC 20005, Tel: 202-626-3780, (www.ctj.org) focuses on tax issues.

Chapter 6: Education and Welfare. In March of every year, the Bureau of the Census (www.census.gov) conducts a survey of U.S. families to determine trends in income and poverty. The results are published annually in the *Current Population Reports* (CPR) Series P-60, often under the title *Money Income of Households, Families, and Persons in the United States*. Recently, the Bureau of the Census began to conduct a survey of income and program participation that includes information about who receives public assistance. Some of the results are published in the CPR Series P-70 *Economic Characteristics of Households in the United States*.

Expenditures per recipient in social programs such as Aid to Families with Dependent Children are published monthly by the Social Security Administration (www.ssa.gov) in the *Social Security Bulletin*; annual figures are summarized in the January *Statistical Supplement*. Excellent data, as well as good arguments, can be found in the publications of the Children's Defense Fund, including a monthly newsletter and a regular report entitled *The State of America's Children*. 25 E Street NW, Washington, DC 20001. Tel: 202-628-8787 (www.childrensdefense.org). For a clearinghouse of information check out the Welfare Information Network at (www.welfareinfo.org).

The Condition of Education and the Digest of Educational Statistics, published by the National Center for Educational Statistics (www.nces.ed.gov), a division of the U.S. Department of Education (www.ed.gov), are good primary sources on the state of education. For both statistics and articles, see *The Chronicle of Higher Education*, published on a weekly basis.

Chapter 7: Health. Primary sources on the health of Americans are *Health, United States* and *Vital Statistics of the U.S.*, both published annually by the National Center for Health Statistics (www.cdc.gov/nchswww) of the U.S. Dept. of Health and Human Services (www.os.dhhs.gov). Information on health care costs and expenditures can be found in the *Health Care Financing Review* (www.hcfa.gov/pubforms/ordpub.htm) which is published by the Health Care Financing Administration (www.hcfa.gov).

Chapter 8: Environment. Many different sources are useful here, but a publication that provides an international overview of the state of the environment is the *World Resources Report*, a joint publication of several international organizations. One of the contributors is the World Resources Institute, or WRI, 10 G St. NE Suite 800, Washington DC, 20002, Tel: 202-729-7600, (www.wri.org). Another contributing organization is the United Nations Environmental Program, or UNEP (www.unep.org). You can find extracts from the 1998-99 *World Resources Report* at www.wri.org/wri/wr-98-99.

Chapter 9: Macroeconomics. The tables published in the back of T*he Economic Report of the President* (www.access.gpo.gov/eop/) are an excellent source of summary statistics. Tables in the monthly *Survey of Current Business*, published by the Department of Commerce (www.doc.gov), and the *Federal Reserve Bulletin*, published by the Board of Governors, Federal Reserve (www.bog.frb.fed.us), provide even more current data. The Bureau of Economic Analysis (www.bea.doc.gov) is responsible for compiling national economic statistics, such as gross domestic product (GDP). The Department of Commerce maintains a website with lots of up-to-date information on the state of the economy called Stat-USA (www.stat-usa.gov).

Cross-national macroeconomic data can be found in *Main Economic Indicators*, published by the Organization for Economic Cooperation and Development, or OECD (www.oecd.org), and in International Financial Statistics (monthly) and *Balance of Payments Yearbook*, published by the International Monetary Fund, or IMF (www.imf.org). The Southern Finance Project keeps abreast of developments in the financial sector in the U.S. and publishes regular briefing papers: P. O. Box 334, Philomont, VA 22131, Tel: 703-338-7754.

Chapter 10: The Global Economy. The May issue of the Commerce Department's *Survey of Current Business* summarizes U.S. international transactions for the preceding year. *The Federal Reserve Bulletin* also includes a great deal of data on foreign trade and exchange rates. *U.S. Industrial Outlook*, a yearly publication of the U.S. Department of Commerce, is a good source of information on the international situation of most U.S. industries. See the Macroeconomics Toolkit Section for contact information.

For information on developing countries, the IMF publications mentioned above are good sources for financial data. For comprehensive information on many aspects of economic development, the World Bank in Washington, DC, publishes annually the *World Development Report* and *World Development Indicators*, which constitute reliable sources for data: The World Bank, 1818 H St. NW, Washington DC, 20433, Tel: (202) 477-1234 (www.worldbank.org).

A more humane approach, oriented toward assessment of human needs, can be found in *The Human Development Report*, an annual publication of the United Nations Development Program (UNDP) (www.undp.org). The United Nations (www.un.org) also publishes the annual *World Economic Survey*, which covers major issues facing the world economy, and, every four years, the *Report on the World Social Situation*.

T.2 How to Read and Write Graphs

Despite the fact that we are bombarded daily by graphs and graphics, it's easy to be intimidated, confused, or misled by them. The best way to learn to read graphs is to make a few. Once you have a sense of how to make them by hand, you might have the inclination and the opportunity to take advantage of modern software for personal computers that allows you to punch them out with abandon. Here are some basic guidelines for reading graphs:

1. Figure out what the variables are. A graph usually displays a relationship between the values of two or more variables. In bar and line graphs, the value of one variable is usually represented on a horizontal axis that starts at zero and increases to the right. The values of other variables are usually represented on a vertical axis that starts at zero and increases upward. For instance, look at Chart 2.6: Along the horizontal axis, time increases from 1950 to 1997. Along the vertical axis, the value of earnings runs from 0 to $8.

    Pie charts picture the relationship between a whole and its parts, as in Chart 3.13. Columns or bars can be used the same way, as in Chart 4.2.
2. Look at the range of the values of the variables: Sometimes they start not at zero but at a higher value, as in Chart 2.4. Often, they are multiples of the numbers indicated, such as thousands or millions. The scale of measurement used largely determines the visual impact of a graph.
3. Ask yourself what you expected the relationship to be. Graphs display patterns. Only a critical, attentive reader can decide whether those patterns really represent important trends.

When you set out to make graphs, follow a similar line of reasoning:

1. Choose the variables whose relationship you want to explore or display; let them determine the type of graph.
2. Decide upon the range and the units you want to use. Experiment with some alternatives, and expect a fair amount of trial and error.
3. Choose the length of your horizontal and vertical axes (or the diameter of your pie). Allow enough space for the variation you want to show. Note that the relative length of the two axes will determine how the graph looks. Increasing the length of the vertical axis will exaggerate differences in the values; increasing the length of the horizontal axis will minimize them.

A computer can do much of the trial-and-error part of this work, though you still have to make the decisions and enter the numbers. The specifics depend almost entirely on the hardware and software you have access to. In general:

1. You need a computer, a printer, and some kind of graphing software. Since most computers come with a suite of business applications pre-installed, chances are good that you already have the software you need. The best place to start is with a spreadsheet program, like Excel, Lotus 123, or Quattro Pro. You may be able to access a graphing module directly from your word processor. Business presentation programs like PowerPoint and

Freelance Graphics can create graphs and combine them with text, illustrations, and a variety of effects to make slideshows.

2. You may find that you need more than one program to do what you need to do. For example, to produce the graphs for this book, we entered data into spreadsheets in Excel and used that program to generate the graphs. Then we copied the graphs into PageMaker, our page layout program. Later, we'll take the same graphs and paste them into the *Field Guide* website (www.fguide.org), using FrontPage, our Web authoring program.

3. The software we've been talking about is getting easier and easier to use; it's made for businesspeople, not techno-geeks. But the more powerful it is, the longer it takes to learn how to make all its features work for you. So ask for help from somebody who knows how to use it. Read the manual if you have to. Give yourself plenty of time to play around and don't worry about making mistakes. It's only numbers.

T.3 Means, Medians, and Other Measures

Sometimes empirical data is wrapped up in a bewildering variety of statistical terms such as "means" and "medians." You can look up their definition in a dictionary or glossary, but the best way to learn what they mean is to apply them yourself. One way of summarizing information about a large number of cases is to ask what's happening to the "typical" case. For instance, you might want to know the income of the typical U.S. family. There are two common but different ways of estimating this.

The simplest and most common way is to calculate the average, also called the "mean." Take the sum of all family income and divide it by the number of families. Another way to define "typical" is by the median, rather than the mean. Line up all the relevant cases from the lowest value to the highest and choose the one that is closest to the middle: the family whose income was greater than the bottom half but lower than the top half.

Sometimes, the mean and the median are the same. More often, they diverge. The reason is that extreme cases affect the mean more than the median. For instance, if you added one family with an income 100 times greater than the next family, it would pull the average up a great deal but change the median hardly at all. The overall distribution of income, like the distribution of both earnings and wealth, has many more extreme cases on the high side than on the low side. For this reason, the mean overestimates the income of the typical family, and the median is a better measure.

T.4 Real vs. Nominal: How to Use Price Indices

Most people think that something that is real is just something that is not imaginary. In the economist's world, however, the word "real" describes a number that has been adjusted to take inflation into account. A real value is one that is expressed in constant dollars, or dollars with the same purchasing power. By contrast, a nominal value reflects the value or purchasing power current at the time and is therefore described as being in "current" dollars.

You can use estimates of the rate of inflation to convert nominal values (expressed in current dollars of purchasing power) to real values (expressed in constant dollars of purchasing power). First, you must decide what estimate of the rate of inflation to use. The most commonly used measure is the Consumer Price Index for urban consumers, or CPI-U. This index calculates the number of dollars required to buy a certain "basket of goods" (including food, clothing, and housing) in a certain benchmark year (or an average of several years), such as 1967, and determines how many dollars would have been required in another year, such as 1998, to purchase the same basket of goods. The ratio between the two determines the CPI-U.

For instance, in 1998, the CPI-U was 163 relative to the benchmark years 1982-84 = 100. That means that $1.63 in 1998 had the same purchasing power as $1 over the years 1982 to 1984. To calculate the value of your 1998 salary of $22,000 in 1982-84 dollars (and determine if your real wages have increased), set up this formula and plug in the appropriate numbers:

$$\frac{1998 \ \text{CPI-U}}{1982\text{-}84 \ \text{CPI-U}} = \frac{\text{your salary in 1998 dollars}}{\text{your salary in 1982-4 dollars}}$$

$$\frac{163}{100} = \frac{\$22,000}{x}$$

Using a little algebra ("crossmultiply and divide"—multiply the 1982-84 CPI-U by the 1998 salary, then divide by the 1998 CPI-U), you can determine that your 1998 earnings have the same purchasing power as $13,496.93 had, on average, over the years 1982 to 1984.

Suppose you want to compare your real earnings in 1990 with your real earnings in 1998. As long as you can consult an estimate of the CPI-U for the range of years you are interested in, you can use any year as a base year. The 1990 CPI-U is 130.7. You can use the figure you just used for 1998 CPI-U to convert your 1998 salary (say, $22,000 again) to 1990 dollars as follows:

$$\frac{163}{130.7} = \frac{\$22,000}{x}$$

A few calculations show that x, your 1998 salary in 1990 dollars, is $17,640.49. Did you earn more or less than that in 1990?

There are a variety of Consumer Price Indices, and the method used to construct them has changed over time. In particular, the Bureau of Labor Statistics (BLS) adjusted the CPI index in 1998, creating a new series. There are a number of reasons for the update, including changes in the quality of goods and services, the need to account for new products which never existed before, and changes in patterns of consumer spending. For more details on these changes, see the CPI website at stats.bls.gov/cpihome.htm.

No index is a perfect measure of the purchasing power of your dollars, because the goods and services you spend money on may be different from those included in the basket of goods the BLS uses.

Another complication is that the composition of the average basket of goods people buy varies over time. The rates of price increase vary considerably—in some years, food prices may increase faster; in some years slower than the cost of other commodities. In addition to the Consumer Price Index for all items, the BLS publishes indices for many separate items.

Many important economic data, such as measurements of gross national product or investment, pertain to sums of money that are not really spent by consumers. To convert these sums to real terms, you should use a different index, the Implicit Price Deflator, which is calculated for this purpose. You can use it exactly the same way as the CPI, using either the overall index or an index of one of its separate components.

T.5 The Census Vocabulary: Families, Households, Persons, and Heads

In the language of the Census Bureau, "person" means just what we expect it to—an individual human being. The official bureau terms "families" and "households," however, mean something a little different from their everyday definitions. A family is any group of people related by blood, marriage, or adoption living at the same residence. If you don't live with your parents, you are not considered part of their family (and the census would not consider your income part of their family income). People who live alone are not considered members of families. By official definition, they represent single-person households.

A household consists of all the people living in one residence, whether or not they are related. Individuals, unrelated roommates, and families all qualify; but people living in "institutions" such as prisons, army barracks, and hospitals are not considered part of households. Here's one way to keep the distinction straight: According to the Census Bu-

reau, all families are households, but not all households are families.

People who compile statistics should choose their units of analysis carefully. Sometimes the choice is obvious. You wouldn't want to ask what percentage of households experienced a divorce because many household members aren't even married. On the other hand, you wouldn't want to ask what percentage of families received Social Security because you would be excluding all people living alone, many of whom are elderly.

At other times, the choice is not so obvious. The percentage of all households that include children is arguably just as interesting a "fact" as the percentage of families that include children. But the two percentages mean different things and should not be confused.

Beyond the household/family distinction lies the question of "headship." Until 1980, the bureau always classified a husband as the head of his family if he lived in the same household. A female-headed family household was, by definition, a family household lacking a husband. Now, the census is more diplomatic and designates the person in whose name the home is owned or rented as the householder. If the home is owned or rented jointly by a married couple, either the husband or the wife may be listed first. The families once termed "female-headed" are now termed "families with female householders, no husband present." The Bureau of Labor Statistics has a nicer way of putting it: "families maintained by women."

T.6 What They Call Us: Racial and Ethnic Labels in Economic Data

Everyone who works with economic statistics about people should pay attention to the implications of racial and ethnic labels. The categories that government agencies such as the Bureau of the Census and the Bureau of Labor Statistics use to define and gather economic data reflect the unspoken assumptions and biases of the larger society. Sometimes, these categories are politically offensive or simply outdated. Sometimes, agencies change and improve the racial and ethnic labels but introduce problems of comparability between data collected in different years. Take, for instance, the category "non-white" which government agencies once used to describe African Americans, Asians, and Native Americans as a group. This category accurately reflects conventional English usage of this period, a usage defined by a white population which automatically considered its own race as the standard. It's a bit like defining women as "non-men."

The conventional racial categories "white" and "non-white" also overlooked the distinctive character and sense of community shared by people whose origins lay in Spanish-speaking countries. In 1979, many government agencies responded to widespread criticism by changing their categories to white, black, and Hispanic (of Spanish origin), providing data for these three groups and largely discontinuing the white/nonwhite distinction. However welcome this change, it made it difficult to construct longrun data series. There is no data predating 1979 for blacks and Hispanics as separate groups, and there is very little data after 1978 for Asians, Native Americans, or people of color as a whole.

The 1990s have witnessed more change and controversy. Many blacks (though not all), preferring to be described according to ethnic heritage, now choose to be called "African Americans." The term "Hispanic" has been criticized because it misleadingly implies Spanish, and thereby European, origin. Perhaps the greatest failing of official terminology is the historical lack of any means of identifying a "multiracial" identity, even though much of the population actually has a mixed heritage.

It is easy to overlook the implications of racial/ethnic distinctions. For instance, you might think that you could arrive at the total number of families in poverty by adding together white families in poverty, African-American families in poverty, and Latino families in poverty. Not so. Latino is an ethnic, not a racial designation. Latinos can be categorized either as black or white; if you add their numbers to the numbers of black and white families, you will over-count the total. At the same time, you will overlook those Asian and Native American families living in poverty.

For the most part, the Census Bureau invites people to define their own race and ethnicity, and there are no hard-and-fast rules for people to follow. For instance, American Indians became more assertive of their cultural pride and political rights in the 1970s, and many people who had never done so before identified themselves as Indians. If you didn't know this, you might infer incorrectly from census publications that American Indians had an extraordinarily high rate of population growth.

Because racial categories change, it is sometimes difficult to follow one series of data over a long period of time. For instance, until 1978 the Handbook of Labor Statistics provided data on average earnings for "Black and other" workers. Beginning in 1979, the category changed to "Black." One might be tempted to splice the two series together. But this would be misleading; "Black and other" included people of Asian origin, whose relatively high incomes raised the average earnings of the group significantly above those of African Americans.

Beginning in the year 2000, the racial and ethnic classifications used by all government agencies will undergo another fundamental shift. There will be five official broad racial classifications: (1) American Indian and Alaskan Native, (2) Black or African-American, (3) Asian, (4) Native Hawaiian or Pacific Islander, and (5) White. For the first time, people will be able to identify with one or more racial category. A "multiracial" category, however, will not be added. There will be two ethnic classifications: (1) Hispanic or Latino and (2) Not Hispanic or Latino. Recommendations to create additional ethnic categories, such as Arab or Middle Eastern, will not be adopted. Furthermore, there will be no provision made for "multi-ethnic" identities. Because of the date of publication, the data used in this book will not reflect this changes. However, these shifts should be kept in mind when comparing pre-2000 and post-2000 statistics by racial and ethnic categories.

No matter how careful you are, you still have to make difficult decisions about how to categorize different groups of people. In this book, we depend upon the racial and ethnic categories used by the government agencies that collect statistical data but sometimes use a different nomenclature. We prefer "African-American" to "black," and "Latino" to "Hispanic," though we occasionally use all four terms. We provide more disaggregated data wherever feasible.

Because we think there is an important political and cultural boundary between whites and a group that includes African Americans, Latinos, Asians, and Native Americans, we use the term "people of color" as an alternative to "non-white." It is an alternative, not a synonym, because it includes Latinos, which "non-white" does not. We use the term "Native Americans" to refer to the group the Bureau of the Census currently labels "American Indians, Eskimos, and Aleuts."

T.7 Measuring Growth: What's Gross About Gross Domestic Product?

When economists use the word "gross," they usually mean "total." Gross domestic product (GDP) is simply the total value of all the goods and services produced for sale within a country (usually in a given year). But there is something a little gross, even downright vulgar, about using GDP as a measure of total production or economic welfare. None of the many goods and services produced in households are included in GDP because they aren't sold. And GDP doesn't reflect changes in the quantity or quality of goods that don't have a price tag, such as clean air or good health. But unless and until a better summary of production is widely adopted, GDP will remain central to the national income accounts that government agencies use to track the growth of the economy over time.

Until recently, the Bureau of Economic Analysis (www.bea.doc.gov) emphasized the gross national product (GNP), or the value of all goods and services produced by U.S. firms or U.S. citizens (whether inside or outside the country).

In 1991, it began to use GDP for two reasons: first, to make U.S. national accounting figures compatible with those of other countries, and, second, because the GDP, in contrast with the GNP, emphasizes production located in the United States, no matter who gets the income from it. In other words, income earned by foreigners on economic activities taking place in the U.S. is included in the GDP, while it is not in the GNP. Similarly, income earned by Americans on investment in foreign countries is not included in the GDP but is a component of the GNP. As the U.S. is getting more and more integrated into the global economy, the GDP gives a more reliable picture of economic activity taking place in the U.S.

The national accounts break GDP down into four components:

1. Goods and services purchased by households and individuals, or personal-consumption expenditures.
2. Those purchased by businesses, or gross private domestic investment, including investment in inventory.
3. Exports minus imports, or net exports (negative in recent years).
4. Government purchases.

Estimates of the value of these items in the national accounts are usually released quarterly by the Bureau of Economic Analysis, often seasonally adjusted and converted to an annual rate in order to make them more easily comparable. A detailed explanation of the national accounts system is provided in *The U.S. Economy Demystified: What the Major Economic Statistics Mean and Their Significance for Business*, by Albert T. Sommers (Lexington, MA: D.C. Heath and Company, 1985).

T.8 Uppers and Downers: The Business Cycle

Economic growth fluctuates, and its ups and downs are usually described as part of a cycle of recession and recovery. Economists declare a recession when GNP declines (in other words, when economic growth is negative) for 2 quarters of a year in a row. A recession year is one in which GNP is lower than it was in the previous year. "Depression" is a word reserved for deep, dark recessions that last a long time. There is no technical definition for a recovery; but the term usually refers to the period immediately after recession, when growth is restored.

Why is the economy plagued by a business cycle? At least a dozen explanations have been offered, including one that blames sunspots. But most economists agree that the business cycle is closely related to fluctuations in the level of business investment. That level is determined by expected costs and expected profits, which shift in both predictable and unpredictable ways.

Because the business cycle has such an important impact on virtually all economic indicators, it's important to keep it in mind when interpreting economic statistics and to distinguish between short-run and long-run trends. Imagine, for instance, a beach at the ocean. If the water is calm and there are no waves, it's easy to tell whether the tide is moving in or out. But a lot of waves can disguise the movement of the tide. To see which way it's going, you might need to compare the distance from peak to peak (or from trough to trough) of several succeeding waves. Economists use the word "secular" to describe trends that are not cyclical.

T.9 A Guide to the Federal Budget

Every January, the president presents a proposed budget for the next fiscal year (FY) to Congress. For example, in January 1998, President Clinton transmitted his budget for fiscal year 1999, which runs from October 1, 1998, to September 30, 1999. This budget presents the administration's proposals for all the different programs of the federal government, including national defense, Social Security, Medicaid, and education. It explains and defends the spending required to meet the administration's objectives in all these areas. It also projects government revenues for the fiscal year and, consequently, the federal deficit.

The president's budget is only a proposal until it is passed by Congress and signed into law by the president. Congressional work on the budget originates in the spring in the House of Representatives. After lengthy work by the House Appropriations Committee, the House votes on an appropriations bill. The approved budget proposal is sent to the Senate, which comes up with its own version. A House and Senate conference committee then works out the differences between the two proposals, and the final bill is sent to the president. The president then has the choice of either signing the bill into law or vetoing it, but he cannot amend it.

The federal budget process has a terminology (as well as a logic) of its own. For instance, there is an important difference between budget authority and outlays. The term "budget authority" describes an amount of money that is authorized for a particular program, which might last for several years. "Outlays" refers to the amount of money spent out of the budget authority "checking account" during a particular fiscal year. When calculating the budget deficit, one must focus on budget outlays. Budget authorities often extend over several budget years; in a given fiscal year, most federal spending is in a sense predetermined by previous budgets. Given the existence of both budget authority and entitlements (such as Social Security, veterans' benefits, and Medicare), only a small component of the federal budget is discretionary in a given budget year.

Economists disagree over the correct definition of the federal deficit. One issue is a component of the budget known as the Social Security Trust Fund, money accumulated to help pay future Social Security claims. This fund currently has a large surplus, which makes the deficit look much smaller. But since it is money that must be spent at some future date, Congress decided it should not be included. The Omnibus Budget Reconciliation Act of 1990 enshrined Social Security as an "off-budget" item, which means it is not counted when calculating the deficit.

For a good discussion of this and other issues surrounding the definition of the deficit, see Robert Eisner, *The Misunderstood Economy: What Counts and How to Count It* (Boston: Harvard Business School Press, 1994).

T.10 Poverty and the Poverty Line

Feeling poor in the U.S. is not the same thing as officially being poor. The U.S. government includes a person or family among the poor if their income falls below an officially designated poverty line or "threshold" that varies according to family size.

In 1998, the poverty threshold for a single person under 65 years old was $8,480; for a family of 4 including 2 children, it was $16,450. Every year, these thresholds are adjusted for inflation. A list of the different poverty thresholds can be found at www.census.gov/hhes/poverty/threshld.html.

This definition of poverty is problematic for a number of reasons. First, the original threshold was set in a somewhat arbitrary way that has become increasingly inaccurate over time. Second, it is misleading to define poverty entirely in absolute, rather than in relative, terms. In 1960, the poverty line for a family of 4 amounted to about 54% of median family income; but by 1998, it had fallen to less than a third. In relative terms, poor families were much poorer in 1998.

These are good reasons to raise the poverty line, but of course, doing so would increase the poverty rate (the percentage of people with incomes below the poverty line). Revisions that would decrease the official poverty rate have received far more recent attention.

Since the mid-1970s, government transfer programs have provided large amounts of noncash or in-kind assistance, such as food stamps, Medicaid, and subsidized housing. It's difficult to estimate the "market value" of such benefits. For instance, if the value of services received through Medicaid were counted as if it were cash income, a person could escape official poverty simply by getting very sick. Still, the failure to include some estimate of noncash transfers in calculations of family income biases the official poverty rate upward. This compensates to some extent for the effect of setting the poverty line very low.

Changes in the definition of the poverty line affect calculations of trends as well as levels of poverty. If the full value of noncash transfers is included in calculations of family income in the 1980s and no other revisions are made, estimates of the poverty rate are lower. However, the estimated increase in the poverty rate between 1980 and 1998 is even greater because cuts in social spending diminished the relative size of noncash transfers to poor people.

For a good discussion of these issues, see Patricia Ruggles, *Drawing the Line: Alternative Poverty Measures and Their Implications for Public Policy* (Washington, DC: The Urban Institute Press, 1990).

Glossary

401(k) Plan. Arrangements that allow employees to make a tax-deferred contribution into a trust in order to finance investments. Employees get their money back when they depart from the plan or upon retirement.

Affirmative action. A plan or program to remedy the effects of past racial or sexual discrimination in employment and to prevent its recurrence. Unlike antidiscrimination or equal opportunity laws, which forbid unequal treatment, affirmative action requires positive corrective measures.

Aid to Families with Dependent Children (AFDC). Financial aid provided under the assistance program of the Social Security Act of 1935 for families of children who lack adequate support but are living with one parent or relative. In 1996, AFDC was replaced by Transitional Assistance for Needy Families (TANF).

Asset. Anything of value that is owned. See *Financial assets*.

Balance of payments. The difference between the total payments into and out of a country during a period of time. It includes such items as all merchandise trade, tourist expenditures, capital movements, and interest charges.

Bond. An IOU or promissory note from a corporation or government. A bond is evidence of a debt on which the issuer (borrower) usually promises to pay a specified amount of interest for a specified period of time and usually to repay the principal on the date of expiration, or maturity date.

Budget deficit. The amount by which government expenditures exceed government tax revenues. The difference must be borrowed.

Budget surplus. The amount by which government tax revenues exceed government expenditures.

Business cycle. The pattern of medium-term economic fluctuations in which expansion is followed by recession, which is followed by expansion, and so on.

Business equity. The total value of a firm's assets, less the amount that is owed to creditors. For corporations, the stock of a company represents a significant portion of its equity.

Capital gain. The difference between the purchase price of an asset and its resale price at some later date. It is called a "capital loss" if the resale price is less than the purchase price.

Capital goods. Machinery, equipment, and structures used in the production of goods and services.

Capital stock. The sum of capital goods in an economy.

Caring labor. Work, both paid and unpaid, that involves face-to-face personal care for other people, including children, elderly individuals, and disabled or sick persons.

Commercial banks. Privately owned banks that receive deposits and make loans. Commercial banks issue time and savings deposits, operate trust departments, act as agents in buying and selling securities, and underwrite and sell new security issues for state and local governments.

Comparable worth. A method for establishing a wage and salary structure across occupations whereby an occupation's wage rate or salary is based on certain characteristics, such as responsibility and working conditions, in comparison with other occupations. Also called *pay equity*.

Conglomerate. A corporation which competes in multiple, not necessarily related industries. A conglomerate often acquires its large, diversified holdings through mergers and/or acquisitions.

Consumer Price Index (CPI). A measure of the average change in prices over time in a fixed "market basket" of goods and services purchased either by urban wage earners and clerical workers (CPI-W) or by all urban consumers (CPI-U).

Corporate income tax. A tax imposed on the annual net earnings of a corporation. In the U.S., such taxes are levied by the federal government and by most states on all incorporated business.

Corporation. A form of business organization consisting of an association of owners, called "stockholders," who are regarded as a single entity (person) in the eyes of the law.

Cost-of-living allowance (COLA). An increase in wages, based on a Consumer Price Index, intended to keep them in line with the current cost of living.

Depreciation. The cost, due to wear and tear, aging, and/or technological obsolescence, of restoring the capital goods used in producing last year's output.

Depression. A prolonged period in which business activity is at a very low level. Production is greatly reduced, there is little or no new capital investment, income is sharply lowered, there is massive unemployment, many businesses fail, and banks are slow to create credit.

Deregulation. The lessening of government control over the operations of various industries.

Devaluation. A reduction in the value of a country's currency relative to foreign currencies.

Discouraged workers. Workers who have become so discouraged by their unsuccessful search for employment that they give up and withdraw from the labor force.

Dividends. A payment to shareholders in a company, in the form of cash or shares, in proportion to their share of ownership.

Dow Jones Industrial Average. An daily index, based on the prices of 30 industrial stocks, that serves as a barometer of the stock market as a whole.

Downsizing. A reduction in the size of a firm's work force.

Employee stock ownership plan (ESOP). Also called "employee stock purchase plan," an ESOP permits employees to purchase stock in the company which employs them, often at a discount from the current market price, by means of payroll deductions. While giving employees partial ownership of the firm's assets, ESOPs usually confer little or no control over them.

Equal Employment Opportunity Commission (EEOC) An independent federal agency established by the Civil Rights Act of 1964 to help end racial and sexual discrimination in employment practices and promote voluntary affirmative action. The EEOC stresses confidential persuasion and conciliation to achieve its objectives. Though given authority in 1972 to institute legal actions if conciliation fails, the EEOC lacks authority to issue cease-and-desist orders.

Equal Pay Act. The 1963 labor law which prohibits discrimination in pay on the basis of race or gender.

Exchange Rate. The price of one currency expressed in terms of another currency, usually the U.S. dollar.

Excise Tax. A tax on the sale of goods. Includes general sales taxes plus other taxes on specific commodities (for example, a cigarette or alcohol tax).

Export. Any good or service sold to a foreign country.

Federal Reserve Bank. The central bank of the United States. Its main purpose is to maintain and enhance the viability and stability of the monetary system. The "Fed" operates under a system of 12 Federal Reserve banks owned by the member banks in their respective districts.

Financial assets. Assets that are financial in character, such as cash, stocks, bonds, or government securities.

Financial Wealth. The total value of financial assets, such as stocks, bonds, and securities, less any outstanding financial obligations, such as loans.

Fiscal policy. The policy of using government spending and taxation to affect some aspect of the economy, especially levels of unemployment and inflation.

Food Stamps. A welfare program to improve nutrition in low-income households. The Food Stamp program is administered by the Department of Agriculture through state and local welfare agencies, which establish eligibility, issue stamps, and maintain controls.

Foreign direct investment (FDI). Investment from abroad that represents a significant degree of managerial influence (usually meaning at least 10% ownership of the voting stock of an enterprise). Foreign direct investment is often assumed to be more long-term and less volatile in nature than other types of foreign investment (see Portfolio Investment).

Greenhouse gasses. A group of gases which accumulate in the atmosphere and appear to contribute to global warming. The gases include carbon dioxide, methane, nitrous oxide, and CFC-12.

Gross Domestic Product (GDP). A measure of the total value of goods and services produced within the country over a specified time period, normally a year. Income arising from investments abroad is not included.

Gross National Product (GNP). A measure of the value of the goods and services produced by the residents of the country (regardless of where the assets are located) over a specified time period, normally a year. It includes income from U.S. investments abroad.

Health Maintenance Organization (HMO). A health care provider that extends coverage for a pre-paid fixed fee. The HMO makes decisions concerning who provides the medical care and when different types of services will be made available.

Householder. The person (or one of the persons) in whose name the housing unit is owned or rented. The U.S. Census describes other members of the household in terms of their relationship to the householder.

Import. Any good or service purchased from a foreign country.

Infant mortality rate. The number of infants per 1,000 born that die within the first year of life.

Inflation. A general increase in prices, often measured by an increase in the Consumer Price Index.

International Monetary Fund. An institution affiliated with the United Nations, set up at the Bretton Woods Conference in 1944 to promote international monetary cooperation, facilitate the growth of international trade, and make the fund's resources available to members.

Investment (capital). A purchase of capital goods that will be used directly in production of goods and services.

Investment (financial). The purchase of any financial

asset, such as a stock or bond. Distinguished from the purchase of productive capital, such as a plant or equipment.

Labor force. Those persons who have jobs or are actively looking for jobs.

Labor force participation rate. The proportion of the working-age population that is part of the labor force.

Labor productivity. The amount of goods or services produced by a worker in a given time period (for example, goods produced per hour of work).

Liabilities. The claims of a creditor. The assets of an individual or business are subject to payment of these claims.

Liberalization. The reduction or removal of government regulations and controls over the exchange of goods, services, and assets, for both domestic and international transactions. Examples of such regulations include tariffs on imports and controls on financial flows.

Macroeconomics. The study of the behavior of the economy as a whole, focusing on variables such as employment, inflation, growth, and stability.

Mean. See *Toolkit*, section T.3.

Median. See *Toolkit*, section T.3.

Medicaid. A federal program that pays for medical services for some low-income households.

Medicare. A health insurance program enacted in 1965 as an amendment to the Social Security Act to provide medical care for the elderly.

Merger. The fusion of two or more separate companies into one.

Microeconomics. The study of individual decision-making in response to changes in prices and incomes.

Minimum wage. The lowest wage, established by federal law, which can be paid by an employer. Some states also have minimum wages.

Monetary policy. The use of monetary controls such as restriction or expansion of the money supply and manipulation of interest rates in order to achieve some desired policy objective, such as the control of inflation, an improvement in the balance of payments, a certain level of employment, or growth in the GNP.

Monopoly. Strictly speaking, a monopoly exists when a firm or individual produces and sells the entire output of some commodity. The lack of competition confers market power on the monopoly firm.

Mortgage. A legal agreement that creates an interest in real estate or transfers title to personal property as security for the payment of a debt. It is often viewed as a claim against or right in property.

Multinational corporation. A company that has operation centers in many countries, as opposed to an international company, which imports or exports goods but has its operation centered in one country.

Mutual fund. A financial institution that manages investments on behalf of its shareholders. Many individuals contribute to the mutual fund, which then directs the pool of money into different investments. The shareholders receive a portion of the total investment income.

Net domestic product. GDP minus depreciation.

Net national product. GNP minus depreciation.

Net worth. The total assets of a person or business less the total liabilities (amounts due to creditors).

Nonfinancial corporate assets. Physical assets (such as plant, equipment, and inventories) and other assets (such as accounts receivable).

Organization for Economic Cooperation and Development (OECD). A 24-member international, intergovernmental agency founded in 1961 to promote policies leading to optimum economic growth, employment, and living standard in member countries while maintaining financial stability. The OECD reviews economic problems of members, conducts research, collects and disseminates statistics on its member countries, and issues publications. It includes 19 European nations, Canada, the U. S., Japan, Australia, and New Zealand.

Pay equity. See *Comparable worth*.

Pension fund. Sums of money laid aside and normally invested to provide a regular income in retirement or in compensation for disablement.

Per capita. A Latin term meaning "for each person."

Political action committee (PAC). A group of people, usually professionals, that lobbies Congress. PACs raise substantial amounts of money for candidates of their choice.

Portfolio investment. Foreign financial investment in stocks, bonds, and securities. Portfolio investment is often assumed to be short-term and highly mobile. (see *foreign direct investment*).

Poverty line. See *Toolkit,* section T.10.

Poverty rate. The percentage of the population with incomes under the poverty line. See *Toolkit,* section T.10.

Preferred Provider Organization (PPO). A health-care plan that contracts with doctors, clinics, and hospitals to provide care for its members. PPOs do not charge a fixed fee. (see *Health Maintenance Organization*).

Private sector. All economic activities that are independent of government control (or outside the *public sector*), carried on principally for profit but also including non-profit organizations directed at satisfying private needs, such as private hospitals and private schools. Included are enterprises owned individually or by groups, and the self-employed.

Productive capacity. The potential output of a business with existing plant, workers, and equipment.

Profit rate. The ratio of a company's profits to the value of its capital stock.

Progressive tax. A tax in which the tax rate rises with income. The income tax is a good example—rates go up (to a certain point) along with the "bracket" one is in.

Protectionism. The policy of imposing import restrictions, such as tariffs (taxes) or quotas (quantity limits) on imported goods in order to protect domestic industries.

Public sector. That part of the economy which is publicly rather than privately owned. It includes all government departments and agencies and all public corporations such as electricity and water boards.

Real earnings. Earnings after the effects of inflation have been taken into account.

Real interest rate. The interest rate minus the anticipated rate of inflation; what a borrower is actually paying for the use of money. See *Toolkit,* section T.4.

Recession. That part or phase of the business cycle in which total output falls; during recession, investment usually declines, and the demand for labor is reduced, so unemployment rises.

Regressive tax. A tax that takes a larger proportion of low incomes than of high incomes. Many taxes on basic goods such as gasoline are regressive because poor people spend a larger percentage of their income on these goods.

Renewable sources of energy. Energy sources that are not depleted by use, such as solar power.

Revenue-neutral. A revenue-neutral tax bill is one that does not affect overall tax revenues.

Savings. All income not spent on goods and services used for current consumption. Both firms and households save.

Security. Any paper asset. Securities include bonds, government debt, and company stock.

Social Security. Officially known as "Old Age, Survivors, and Disability Insurance" ("OASDI"), its major purposes are to provide retirement income for the elderly, assistance for workers who are totally disabled, income for spouses and children of deceased wage earners, and Medicare. All eligible workers are required to contribute a certain percentage of their earnings, to be matched by their employer.

Stock Option. An agreement allowing a person to purchase a company's stock, often at a favorable price. Usually offered as part of a salary-and-benefits package.

Stocks. Certificates or claims of ownership interests in a corporation. Stocks entitle the owner to dividend payments from the corporation.

Tax loophole. A legal provision that can be used to reduce one's tax liability. Such provisions may be unintentional discrepancies or provisions intended to benefit an industry or group.

Terms of trade. The purchasing power of a country's exports in terms of the imports that they will buy.

Trade deficit. The amount by which a nation's imports exceed its exports of merchandise over a given period.

Temporary Assistance for Needy Families (TANF). A government program to provide short-term aid to low-income families. The program includes term limits on the total length of time assistance can be provided. TANF also requires that participants find employment or be placed in unpaid jobs. TANF replaced Aid to Families with Dependent Children (AFDC) in 1996.

Underemployment. A situation in which an individual, who would like a secure full-time job, is employed only part-time or temporarily.

World Bank. An institution affiliated with the United Nations and set up at the Bretton Woods Conference in 1944, whose chief purpose is to assist in the reconstruction and development of its poor members by facilitating capital investment, making loans, and promoting foreign investment.

World Trade Organization (WTO). An international institution established in 1995 to govern trade agreements, regulatory standards, tariff levels, and intellectual property rights. The WTO renders decisions regarding disputes between member countries. The WTO is located in Geneva, Switzerland.

Sources

For a general guide to sources, see Toolkit, T.1. This list uses the following abbreviations:

BC   U.S. Bureau of the Census
BEA   Bureau of Economic Analysis
BLS   U.S. Bureau of Labor Statistics
BW   *Business Week* (weekly)´
CPR   *Current Population Report,* BC (semimonthly)
DHHS   U.S. Department of Health and Human Services
DS   *Dollars and Sense* (monthly)
EE   *Employment and Earnings,* U.S. Dept. of Labor (monthly)
EPI   Economic Policy Institute, Washington, DC
ERP   *Economic Report of the President,* President's Council of Economic Advisors (annual)
HDR   *Human Development Report,* United Nations Development Program
HT   *Historical Tables,* Budget of U.S. Government
HUS   *Health, United States* (annual) Dept. of Health and Human Services
NIPA   *National Income and Product Accounts,* U.S. Department of Commerce, Bureau of Economic Analysis
NYT   *New York Times* (daily)
OECD   Organization for Economic Cooperation and Development
SA   *Statistical Abstract of the U.S.,* BC (annual)
SCB   *Survey of Current Business,* U.S. Dept. of Commerce
SWA   Lawrence Mishel and Jared Bernstein, *The State of Working America,* EPI Series (Armonk, NY: M.E. Sharpe, annual)
TE   *The Economist* (weekly)
UNCTAD United Nations Committee for Trade and Development
UN   United Nations
WDI   World Bank, *World Development Indicators*
WP   *Washington Post* (daily)
WR   World Resources Institute, UN Environment Programme, UN Development Programme, and the World Bank, *World Resources 1998-99* (New York: Oxford University Press, 1998).
WSJ   *Wall Street Journal* (daily, except weekends)

Chapter 1: Owners

1.1   Edward Wolff, "Recent Trends in the Size Distribution of Household Wealth," *Journal of Economic Perspectives* 12, no. 3 (Summer 1998), pp. 131-50. Edward Wolff, "Recent Trends in Wealth Ownership," manuscript, New York University, 1999, Table 2.
1.2   Wolff, "Recent Trends in Wealth Ownership," Table 2.
1.3   Ibid.
1.4   Ibid. Wolff, "Recent Trends in Wealth Ownership," Table 6.
1.5   *Forbes,* 7/5/99, pp. 220, 222; 7/6/98, pp. 250, 252.
1.6   *HDR* 1998, p. 30, Box 1.3.
1.7   United For a Fair Economy, *Born on Third Base: The Sources of Wealth of the 1997 Forbes 400.* Available from UFE, 37 Temple Place, Fifth Floor, Boston, MA 02111 (www.stw.org).
1.8   *BW,* 4/20/98, pp. 64-70. *BW,* 4/19/99, pp. 72-90. *EE* 46, no. 1

(Jan. 1999), p. 49, Table B-2. Text: *NYT*, 9/3/98, pp. C-1, C-4.

1.9 *Historical Income Tables - Households.* Tables H-1, H-3. (www.census.gov/pub/hhes/income/histinc/h01.html, www.census.gov/pub/hhes/income/histinc/h03.html.)

1.10 *Money Income in the United States, 1997* (CPR P60-200), p. 42, Table 11. Social Security Administration, "Fast Facts About Social Security," July 1998, p. 5.

1.11 Center for Responsive Politics (www.opensecrets.org/pubs/bigpicture/blio/bpblioindiv.html; www.opensecrets.org/pubs/bigpicture/blio/bpbliopac.html). Text: "Industry/Interest Group Contributions in 1997-98" (www.opensecrets.org/pubs/whopaid/bigpic/sum06.htm).

1.12 Center for Responsive Politics, "Campaign Statistics at a Glance" (www.opensecrets.org/pubs/bigpicture/bpstats.html).

1.13 "The Fortune Global 500," *Fortune*, 8/4/97, pp. F-1, F-2. World Bank, *World Development Indicators, 1998*, Table 1.1. Text: Robert McChesney. "The Global Media Giants." *Extra!*, Jan. 1999 (www.fair.org/extra/9711/gmg.html.)

1.14 "The Year of the Mega-Merger," *Fortune*, 1/11/99, p. 62. "Exxon and Mobil announce $80 billion deal," *NYT*, 12/2/98, p. A-1. "The Return of Big Oil," *The Progressive*, Jan. 1999, p. 7. "Citigroup: Scenes From a Merger," *Fortune*, 1/11/99, p. 76. "Citigroup to cut 6% of its work force," *WSJ*, 12/16/98, p. A-8. "Banks Merged," *The Economist.* 8/22/98, p. 5. "It's a Bank-Eat-Bank World." *DS*, Jan/Feb 1999, pp. 11-13, 40. "Maximum Merger" *U.S. News and World Report*, 5/18/98, p. 45. "The First Global Car Colossus," *BW*, 5/18/98, p. 40.

1.15 Laura Colby, "The Fortune Global 500: the world's largest corporations," *Fortune*, 8/4/97, p. F-1.

1.16 National Center for Employee Ownership, "A Statistical Profile of Employee Ownership," Jan. 1999. (www.nceo.org/library/control_eq.html) (www.nceo.org/library/eo_stat.html)

Chapter 2: Workers

2.1 *ERP* 1999, p. 373, Table B-39.

2.2 BLS ftp://ftp.bls.gov/pub/special.requests/ee/ceseeb1.txt, ftp://ftp.bls.gov/pub/special.requests/ee/ceseeb2.txt. Text: BEA Industry Economics Division. "Estimates of Gross Product Originating and the Components of Gross Domestic Product, 1947-97," July 1998.

2.3 BLS, *Employment, Hours, and Earnings, 1909-84*, vol. 2 (Bulletin 1312-12). *EE* 46, no. 1 (Jan. 1999), p.49, Table B-2. CPI-U: BLS website, derived from stats.bls.gov/top20.html

2.4 *Handbook of Labor Statistics 1980* (Bulletin 2070), table 60, p. 118. *Handbook of Labor Statistics 1985* (Bulletin 2217), Table 41, p. 94. *EE*, Jan. issues, 1985-94, table 54. *EE*, Jan. issues 1994-98, Table 37. Note: Before 1979, no data were collected specifically for Hispanics/Latinos. CPI-U: BLS website, derived from stats.bls.gov/top20.html

2.5 *SWA* 1998-99, p. 161, Table 3.22.

2.6 *SA 1993*, p 429, table 675. *SA 1998*, p. 433, Table 674. CPI-U: BLS website, derived from stats.bls.gov/top20.html (1998 based on Jan.-Nov. average).

2.7 BLS Bulletin 2281, *Employee Benefits in Medium and Large Firms, 1986*. BLS News Release, 1/7/99, "Employee Benefits in Medium and Large Private Industry Establishments, 1997" (stats.bls.gov/special.requests/ocwc/oclt/ebs/ebnr0005.pdf). BLS, *Employee Benefits in Small Private Establishments, 1996* (stats.bls.gov/special.requests/

ocwc/oclt/ebs/sml96.pdf).

2.8   *SWA* 1998-99, p. 132, Table 3.7; p. 133, Table 3.8.

2.9   BLS Report 918, "A Profile of the Working Poor, 1996," http://stats.bls.gov/cpswp96.htm. "Health Insurance Coverage: 1997" (CPR P60-202).

2.10   "Living Wage Successes: A Compilation of Living Wage Policies on the Books." Association of Community Organizations for Reform Now (ACORN), May 1999 (www.livingwagecampaign.org/living-wage-wins.html).

2.11   BLS, *Employment Situation*, 11/1/98 (stats.bls.gov/news.release/empsit.toc.htm). Text: BLS. "Contingent and Alternative Employment Arrangements, Feb. 1997." BLS Press Release, 12/2/97 (stats.bls.gov/news.release/conemp.nws.htm).

2.12   *EE*, Dec 1998, Tables A-10, A-11.

2.13   *ERP* 1999, p. 368, Table B-35.

2.14   Gene Koretz, "Downsizing's Economic Spin and Its Impact on Job-losers", *BW*, 12/28/98, derived from BLS, ftp://146.142.4.23/pub/news.release/disp.txt, 8/19/98. Text: *The Downsizing of America* (New York: Times Books, 1996). Gene Koretz, "Will Downsizing Ever Let Up?" *BW*, 2/16/98, p. 26. Martha Groves, "Downsizing Wave has Reached a Point of Diminishing Returns," *Los Angeles Times*, 7/7/96.

2.15   *EE* 46, no. 1 (Jan. 1999), p. 219, Table 40; p. 221, Table 42.

2.16   BLS News Release, "Major Work Stoppages, 1998," 2/10/99 (stats.bls.gov/news.release/wkstp.t01.htm).

Chapter 3: Women

3.1   *ERP* 1999, p. 374, Table B-40. BLS, "Labor Force Statistics Derived From the Current Population Survey: A Databook," vol. 1 (Bulletin 2096), Sept. 1982, p. 716, table C-11. *SA 1986*, p. 399, Table 675. *SA 1994*, p. 402, Table 626. *SA 1997*, p. 404, Table 631. *SA 1998*, p. 409, Table 654.

3.2   *SA 1994*, p. 58, Table 66. *SA 1998*, p. 61, Table 69. Text: "Household and Family Characteristics, March, 1997," (CPR P20-509), p.4, Table B.

3.3   *EE* 28, no. 1 (Jan. 1981), p. 81, Table A-77. *EE* 37, no. 1 (Jan. 1990), p. 79, Table A-73. *EE* 46, no. 1 (Jan. 1999), p. 212, Table 37.

3.4   BLS, ftp:ftp.bls.gov/pub/special.requests/lf/aat39.txt. Text: Richard W. Stevenson, "Texaco is Said to Set Payment Over Sex Bias," *NYT*, 1/6/99. Peter Truell, "A deal reached in a Merrill case may change how the industry handles employees' bias complaints." *NYT*, 5/6/98.

3.5   *1970 U.S. Census, U.S. Summary*, sec. 2, pp. 718-24, Table 21. *1980 U.S. Census*, pt. 1-A, pp. 166-75, Table 276. *EE* 38, no. 1 (Jan. 1991), p. 37, Table A-22. *EE* 46, no. 1 (Jan. 1999), p. 30, Table A-19.

3.6   Annual census of women corporate officers in Fortune 500 companies by Catalyst, New York, (212) 514-7600. *Boston Globe*, 10/10/98, D-15. Text: Kathleen Morris, "You've Come a Short Way, Baby," *BW*, 11/23/98, p. 82.

3.7   BLS, "Median usual weekly earnings" (ftp:ftp.bls.gov/pub/special.requests/lf/aat39.txt).

3.8   Center for the Child Care Workforce (www.ccw.org), "Current Data on Child Care Salaries and Benefits in the U.S.," March, 1998. Text: Child Care Bureau, "A Profile of the Child Care Work Force" (www.acf.hdds.gov/programs/ccb/faq/workforce.htm).

3.9   *CPR*, P60-115, July 1978 , Cover. *Poverty in the U.S.: 1992* (*CPR*, P60-185), p. 1, Table 1. *Poverty in the U.S.: 1997* (*CPR*, P60-201), p. vii, Table A.

3.10   Elaine Sorensen and Ariel Halpern, "Child Support Is

Working Better Than We Think," Number A-31 in Series "New Federalism: Issues and Options for States," Washington: Urban Institute (http://newfederalism.urban.org).

3.11 Ellen Galinsky and Jennifer E. Swanberg, "Employed Mothers and Fathers in the United States: Understanding How Work and Family Life Fit Together," Families and Work Institute 1998, p. 15. Harriet B. Presser, "Employment Schedules Among Dual-Earner Spouses and the Division of Labor by Gender," *American Sociological Review 59* (June 1994), pp. 348-69.

3.12 James T. Bond, Ellen Galinsky, and Jennifer E. Swanberg, *The 1997 National Study of the Changing Workforce* (New York: Families and Work Institute, 1998). Robert Wood Johnson Foundation, *Chronic Care in America: A 21st Century Challenge, 1996* (www.rwf.org.library/chrcare/p3pg30.htm).

3.13 James T. Bond, Ellen Galinsky, & Jennifer E. Swanberg, *The 1997 National Study of the Changing Workforce* (New York: Families and Work Institute, 1998), p. 50. Text: The Children's Defense Fund, *The State of America's Children* (Boston: Beacon Press, 1998).

3.14 Kirstin Grimsley, "Study: U.S. Mothers Face Stingy Maternity Benefits," *WP*, 2/16/98, p. A-10. Sheila Kamerman and Alfred Kahn, *Child Care, Parental Leave and the Under 3s: Policy Innovation in Europe* (New York: Auburn House, 1991). L.A. Whittington, "Taxes and the Family: The Impact of the Tax Exemption for Dependents on Marital Fertility," *Demography 29*, no. 2 (1992), pp. 215-26.

3.15 Tamar Lewin, "Teen-Age Pregnancy Rate at 20-year Low," *NYT* 10/15/98. Alan Guttmacher Institute, "Teen Sex and Pregnancy" (www.agi-usa.org/pub/fb_teen_sex.html).

3.16 Alan Guttmacher Institute, press release (www.agi-usa.org/new/archive/newsrelease3006.htm). "Violence Against Abortion Doctors," *NYT*, 10/26/98. Guttmacher Institute, "Teen Sex and Pregnancy" (www.agi-usa.org/pubs/fb_teensex.html).

Chapter 4: People of Color

4.1 *SA 1997*, p.19, Table 19.

4.2 *SA 1993*, p. 18, Table 18. *Population Projections of the United States, By Age, Sex, Race, and Hispanic Origin, 1995 to 2050* (CPR P25-1130), Feb. 1996, pp. 16-17, Table M.

4.3 *SA 1998*, p. 10, Table 5.

4.4 Douglas S. Massey and Mary J. Fischer, "Where We Live, in Black and White," *The Nation*, 12/14/98, p. 25. Peter Applebome, "Schools See Re-emergence of 'Separate but Equal,'" *NYT*, 4/8/97, p. A10. See also Douglas Massey and Nancy Denton, *American Apartheid: Segregation and the Making of the Underclass* (Cambridge: Harvard University Press, 1993).

4.5 *Handbook of Labor Statistics*, Bulletin 2217, pp. 69-73, Table 27. *EE*, Jan. issues, 1986-94, Table A-63. *EE*, Jan. 1995-98, Table D-16. *EE* Jan. 1999, p. 156, Table D-17. Text: Rochelle Sharpe, "In Latest Recession, Only Blacks Suffered Net Employment Loss," *WSJ* 9/14/93, p. A1.

4.6 *EE* 40, no. 1 (Jan. 1993), p. 22, table A-7. *EE* 41, no. 1 (Jan. 1994), p. 22, Table A-7.

4.7 *SA 1998*, p. 167, Table 260. Text: *Highlights of Educational Attainment in the United States: March 1998* (*CPR*, P20-513).

4.8 *EE* 46, no. 1 (Jan. 1999), p. 153, Table D-14.

4.9 *SA 1984*, p. 434, table 716. *EE* 46, no. 1 (Jan. 1999), p. 159, Table D-20.

4.10 *Poverty in the US: 1997* (*CPR*, P60-201), p. C-2, Table C-1.

4.11 Bureau of Justice Statistics (www.ojp.usdoj.gov/bjs) *Sourcebook of Criminal Justice Statistics, 1997*, p. 480, Table 6.22. Bureau of Justice Statistics, *Corrections Populations in the United States, 1995* (www.ojp.usdoj.gov/bjs/pub/pdf/cpius95.pdf), p. 7, Table 1.6.

4.12 *Population Projections of the United States by Age, Sex, Race, and Hispanic Origin: 1995 to 2050* (CPR, P25-1130), p. 43, Table 2. Bureau of Justice Statistics, *Correctional Populations in the U.S., 1995*, Table 1.6 (www.ojp.usdoj.gov/bjs/pub/pdf/cpius95.pdf). *EE* 43, no. 1 (Jan. 1996), p.162, Table 3. Text: Richard Morin, "Men, Women, and Marriage," *WP*, 12/5/93, p. C2.

4.13 *SA 1985*, p. 47, Table 66. *SA 1998*, p. 65, Table 77.

4.14 *Household and Family Characteristics: March 1998* (*CPR* P20-515), p. 81, Table 8.

4.15 David Blanchflower, Phillip Levine, and David Zimmerman, "Discrimination in the Small Business Credit Market," National Bureau of Economic Research (www.nber.org) Working Paper 6840, Dec. 1998, p. 32, Table 1.

4.16 DeWayne Wickham, "Affirmative Action Not in Real Jeopardy," *U.S.A. Today*, 4/7/98, p. 13A. Ethan Bronner, "Study Strongly Supports Affirmative Action in Admissions to Elite Colleges," *NYT*, 9/9/98. Steven A. Holmes, "The Nation: Re-rethinking Affirmative Action," *NYT*, 4/5/98. Christy Hope, "Official Attributes Growth to New Admission Law," *Dallas Morning News*, 5/20/98.

Chapter 5: Government

5.1 *HT 2000*, p. 200, Table 15.2. BEA, "GDP News Release of April 30, 1999". Text: *HT 2000*, p. 279, Table 17.5.

5.2 OECD, *OECD Economic Outlook*, Dec. 1998, p. 252, Annex Table 28.

5.3 *HT 2000*, p. 42, Table 3.1.

5.4 *SA 1994*, p. 334-35, Table 509. *SA 1998*, p. 342, Table 543.

5.5 National Priorities Project (www.natprior.org) "Are You Winning Or Losing?" p. 28. Federation of American Scientists, "1998 Top Ten & Dirty Dozen," p. 1 (www.fas.org/pub/gen/mswg/msbb98/index.html).

5.6 Data prepared 2/27/98 by Chris Hellman, Senior Research Analyst, Center For Defense. Information from International Institute for Strategic Studies publication, *The Military Balance 1996-1997*. US figure is from Dept. of Defense News Release #026-98, 2/2/98.

5.7 *HT 2000*, p. 21, Table 1.2.

5.8 *HT 2000*, p. 110, Table 7.1. Text: *ERP* 1999, p. 420, Table B-79.

5.9 *HT 2000*, p. 29, Table 2.2.

5.10 Citizens for Tax Justice, *Who Pays, A Distributional Analysis of the Tax Systems in All 50 States*, Appendix 1, p. 52 (www.ctj.org/html/whopay.htm).

5.11 *HT 2000*, p. 29, Table 2.2.

5.12 *Public Citizen News* 18, no. 6 (Nov./Dec. 1998), p. 8. *NYT*, 4/21/99, p. A-17. Text: Center for Responsive Politics, "Influence, Inc." (www.opensecrets.org/lobbyists/).

5.13 Federal Election Commission, "Voter Registration and Turnout" (www.fec.gov/pages/96to.htm, www.fec.gov/votregis/turn/natto.htm).

5.14 "The Congressional Progressive Caucus 'Most Wanted' List of Corporate Welfare 'Fat Cat' Cuts and Alternative Priorities," *Disgruntled* web magazine (www.disgruntled.com/corpwelf.html). Text: Cato Foundation, *Cato Handbook for Congress* (available at www.cato.org). Paulette Olson and Dell Champlin, "Ending Corporate Welfare as We Know It: An Institutional Analysis of the Dual Structure of Welfare," *Journal* of *Economic Issues* 32 (9/1/98), pp. 759-62.

5.15   *ERP* 1999, p. 421, Table B-80. Text: *U.S. News and World Report*, 3/8/99. p. 76. *Fast Facts and Figures About Social Security, 1998*, Social Security Administration, Office of Research, Evaluation, and Statistics, p. 30.

5.16   Century Foundation, "Issue Brief #3" (www.tcf.org/ issue_briefs/social_security/index.html).

Chapter 6: Education and Welfare

6.1   BC, "Historical Income Tables—Families," (www.census.gov/hhes/income/histinc/f07.html).

6.2   *Money Income in the US: 1997* (*CPR*, P60-200), p. B-6, Table B-3. Text: "Inequality Hurts," *BW*, 8/15/94, pp. 78-84. Richard Freeman, "Toward an Apartheid Economy?" *Harvard Business Review*, 9/1/96.

6.3   "The 1998 HHS Poverty Guidelines," *Federal Register* 63, no. 36 (2/24/98), pp. 9235-9238 (excerpted in aspe.hhs.gov/ poverty/98poverty.htm). Patricia Ruggles, *Drawing the Line. Alternative Poverty Measures and Their Implications for Public Policy* (Washington, D.C.: The Urban Institute, 1990).

6.4   *Poverty in the U.S. 1997* (*CPR*, P60-201), p. C-9, Table C-3; p. C-2, Table C-1. Text: Richard F. Wertheimer, "Working Poor Families with Children" (www.childtrends.org/ workingpoor.shtml).

6.5   BC, "Historical Poverty Tables—People" (www.census.gov/ hhes/poverty/histpov/hstpov3.html). Text: "In Debate on U.S. Poverty, Two Studies Fuel the Argument on Who is to Blame," *NYT*, 10/29/91, p. A-20. Editorial, "And Now—Social Security," *TN*, 3/15/99, p. 3.

6.6   DHHS, Trends in the Well-Being of America's Children and Youth, 1998. Greg J. Duncan and Jeanne Brooks-Gunn, "Making Welfare Reform Work for Our Youngest Children," *News and Issues, National Center for Children in Poverty*, Spring 1998, pp. 4-5 (cpmcnet.columbia.edu/ dept/nccp/). The Urban Institute, *National Survey of America's Families, Snapshots* (newfederalism.urban.org/ nsaf/foreword.html).

6.7   *SA 1997*, p. 338, Table 521. *SA 1998*, p. 379, Table 605; p. 118, Table 164. Text: Citizens for Tax Justice, "The Hidden Entitlements," part 3-1. (www.ctj.org/hid_ent/part-3/ part3-1.htm).

6.8   Randy Albelda and Nancy Folbre, *The War on the Poor: A Defense Manual* (New York: The New Press, 1996). Children's Defense Fund, *The State of America's Children* (Boston: Beacon Press, 1998), pp. 7-12. DHHS, "Change In Welfare Caseloads Since Enactment of New Welfare Law" (www.acf.dhhs.gov/news/stats/aug-sep.htm).

6.9   Children's Defense Fund, "Welfare to What? Early Findings on Family Hardship and Well-Being," Dec. 1998 (www.childrensdefense.org/fairstart_welfare2what.html).

6.10   Second Harvest, *Hunger 1997: The Faces and Facts*, Tables 8-26, 8-66 (www.secondharvest.org/research/ faces/ffhome.htm). Text: Andrew C. Revkin, "A Plunge in the Use of Food Stamps Causes Concern," *NYT*, 2/25/99. "Welfare Policies Alter the Face of Food Lines," *NYT*, 2/26/99.

6.11   Michael Janofsky, "The Dark Side of the Economic Expansion," *NYT*, 4/1/99. Report cited: Dept of Housing and Urban Development, "Waiting in vain: an update on America's rental housing crisis" (www.huduser.org/ publications/affhsg/waiting/sect_iii.html), 4/1/99. Text: Jason De Parle, "In Booming Economy, Poor Still Struggle to Pay the Rent," *NYT*, 6/16/98. Jennifer Daskal,

"In Search of Shelter: The Growing Shortage of Affordable Rental Housing," (Washington: Center on Budget and Policy Priorities, 1998-www.cbpp.org/615hous.htm). Michael Janofsky, "The Dark Side of the Economic Expansion," *NYT*, 4/1/99.

6.12   Nicole M. Christian, "Study Offers New Insight on Homeless," *NYT*, 11/1/98. U.S. Conference of Mayors, "Status Report on Hunger and Homelessness, 1998" (order from www.usmayors.org).

6.13   "What Does it Cost to Mind our Preschoolers?" (*CPR*, P70-52), p. 4, Figure 3; p. 5, Table 3. DHHS, Child Care Bureau (www.acf.dhhs.gov/programs/ccb/faq/quality.htm). "Cost, Quality, and Child Outcomes in Child Care Centers," University of Colorado at Denver, 1995. Ruby Takanishi, "Children in Poverty. Reflections on the Roles of Philanthropy and Public Policy," in *Philanthropy and the Nonprofit Sector in a Changing America*, ed. Charles T. Clotfelder and Thomas Erlich (Bloomington, IN: Indiana University Press, 1999, pp. 347-63).

6.14   NEA, "Estimates of School Statistics 1995-96," p. 48, Table 10 (available from www.nea.org/publications). Text: Gene Koretz, "Economic Trends," *BW*, 4/5/99.

6.15   *Digest of Education Statistics*, 1997 (http://nces.ed.gov/pubs/digest97/d97t312.html). Text: Charles T. Clotfelter, "The Familiar But Curious Economics of Higher Education: Introduction to a Symposium," *Journal of Economic Perspectives* 13, no. 1 (Winter 1999), pp. 3-12. Gordon C. Winston, "Subsidies, Hierarchy, and Peers: The Awkward Economics of Higher Education," *Journal of Economic Perspectives* 13, no. 1 (Winter 1999), pp. 13-36.

6.16   Sondra Beverly, "Rich Kids, Poor Kids: the Education Gap is Widening," *St. Louis Post-Dispatch*, 4/29/97.

Chapter 7: Health

7.1   *HUS 1998* (www.cdc.gov/nchswww/products/pubs/pubd/hus/hus.htm), p. 342, Table 116. Text: *Health Insurance Coverage, 1997* (CPR P60-202), p. 1, Fig. 1.

7.2   *HUS 1998*, p. 342, Table 116. Annemarie Muth, ed, *Statistical Abstract of the World*, 3rd Edition (Detroit: Gale Research, 1997) pp. 44, 169, 331, 366, 475, 902, 993. Text: Gene Koretz, "The unhealthy U.S. income gap," *BW*, 11/10/97, p. 22. Richard Wilkinson, *Unhealthy Societies: The Afflictions of Inequality* (New York: Routledge, 1997).

7.3   *HUS 1998*, p. 348, Table 121. Text: *BW*, 10/12/98. p. 144. Note: Total excludes non-patient revenues of $24.7 billion.

7.4   BLS, Consumer Expenditure Survey, "Standard Bulletin Tables 1997, Quintiles of Income Before Taxes" (http://stats.bls.gov/csxstnd.htm#1997). Text: BLS. Consumer Expenditure Survey, "Standard Bulletin Tables 1997," (http://stats.bls.gov/csxhome.htm).

7.5   *SA 1980*, p. 487, Table 808. *SA 1994*, p. 489, Table 748. *SA 1998*, p. 490, Table 773. Text: "Health Care Costs: On the Critical List," *TE*, 2/13/1999, p. 65.

7.6   *SA 1992*, p. 114, Table 170. *SA 1997*, p. 129, Table 188. Text: *HUS 1998*, p. 316, Table 94.

7.7   American Medical Association, *Socioeconomic Characteristics of Medical Practice* 1984, Table 41; 1993, Table 53; 1997/98, p. 112, Table 51. Cpi-u-x1 derived from stats.bls.gov/top20.html. Text: James Moser, "Physician Income Trends in the Last 10 Years," in AMA *Socio-Economic Characteristics of Medical Practice 1997/98*.

7.8   *Fortune*, annual Fortune 500 issue, various years (usually late April). Text: *WSJ* 11/17/98. p. 1.

7.9 Urban Institute, National Survey of American Families, April 1999. "To Get or Skip Care? Coverage Makes the Difference," *Managed Care Magazine*, Dec. 1998, p. 48 (www.managedcaremag.com).

7.10 *HUS 1998*, Table 133, pp. 362-63. Text: *Health Insurance Coverage 1997* (*CPR*, P60-202), p. 1, Fig. 1; p. 5, Table 1.

7.11 *Health Insurance Coverage 1997* (*CPR*, P60-202), p. 2, Fig. 2. Text: *HUS 1998*, p. 200, Table 29; p. 203, Table 31.

7.12 *HUS 1976-77*, p. 166, Table 22. *HUS 1983*, p. 182, Table 11. *HUS 1990*, p. 68, Table 16. *HUS 1998*, p. 193, Table 23. Text: *HUS 1998*, p. 176, Table 6; p. 197, Table 27.

7.13 Larry Levitt and Janet Lundy, "Trends and Indicators in the Changing Health Care Marketplace," Kaiser Family Foundation, August 1998 (www.kff.org/archive/health_policy/market/trends/trends.pdf). Text: "HMO Mergers Signal Higher Medical Costs," *U.S. News and World Report*, 11/21/98, p. 14.

7.14 "Health Care Costs: On the Critical List," *TE*, 2/13/1999, p. 65. "Reality of HMO System Does Not Live Up to Hopes for Health Care," *NYT*, 10/5/98. "Clinically, for-profits lag not-for-profits." *Managed Care Magazine*, Nov. 1998, pp. 42-44 (www.managedcaremag.com).

7.15 World Bank, *World Development Indicators 1998*, p. 92, Table 2.14. Text: *HDR* 1998, pp. 67-68; pp. 158-59, Table 13.

7.16 UNAIDS: The Joint UN Programme on HIV/AIDS , *AIDS Epidemic Update: December 1998* (www.us.unaids.org/highband/document/epidemio/index.html)

Chapter 8: Environment

8.1 Clifford Cobb, Ted Halstead, and Jonathan Rowe, "The Genuine Progress Indicator: Summary of Data and Methodology;" and Jonathan Rowe and Mark Anielski, "The Genuine Progress Indicator: 1998 Update—Data & Methodology," both available from Redefining Progress (www.rprogress.org/pubs/publist.html). Text: Jonathan Rowe and Judith Silverstein, "The GDP Myth," *The Washington Monthly* 31, no. 3 (March 1999).

8.2 *WR*, "Valuing Ecosystem Services," (www.wri.org/wri/wr-98-99/ecoserv.htm). R. Costanza et al, "The Value of the World's Ecosystem Services and Natural Capital," *Nature* 387 (May, 1997), pp. 253-60.

8.3 Loren McArthur and Marc Breslow, "Polluters and Politics," *DS*, July/August 1998, p. 43.

8.4 *SA 1993*, p. 227, Table 372. *SA 1998*, p. 243, Table 402.

8.5 James Hamilton, "Testing for Environmental Racism: Prejudice, Profits, Political Power?" *Journal of Policy Analysis and Management* 14, no. 1, pp. 107-35. Pratap Chatterjee, "Toxic Racism," *DS*, May/June 1997, pp. 13-15. "A Green Bottom Line," *Newsweek*, 11/2/98, p. 53.

8.6 *SA 1998*, p. 246, Table 407. Text: "Changing Environments, Changing Health. Industrialization Overview," *WR* (www.wri.org/wri/wr-98-99/002-ndus.htm). *SA 1998*, p. 245, Table 405. Center for Responsive Politics, "Cashing In" (www.opensecrets.org/pubs/cashingin_104th/40super.html).

8.7 *SA 1985*, p. 199, Table 340. *SA 1990*, p. 202, Table 347. *SA 1997*, p. 233, Table 376. Text: *WR* (www.wri.org/wri/wr-98-99/freshwat.htm).

8.8 *SA 1998*, p. 246, Table 408. *WR*, "Wasting the Material World: The Impact of Industrial Economies" (www.wri.org/wri/wr-98-99/wasting.htm).

8.9 *SA 1993*, p. 332, Table 514. *SA 1998*, p. 341, Table 542. Deflator; *SCB* 78, no. 8, p. 159, Table 3. 1997 estimated.

8.10 R. Schmalensee et. al. "An Interim Evaluation of Sulfur

Dioxide Emissions Trading," *Journal of Economic Perspectives* 12, no. 3 (Summer 1998), pp. 53-68.

8.11　American Automobile Manufacturers Association, "Motor Vehicle Facts and Figures 1997." Text: *HDR 1998*, p. 2. *WR*, "Proceed With Caution: Growth in the Global Motor Vehicle Fleet" (www.wri.org/wri/wr-98-99/autos.htm).

8.12　*SA 1997*, p. 589, Table 934. Text: *WDI* 1998, pp. 150-53, Table 3.9. *HDR* 1998, p. 4.

8.13　*WR*, "Deforestation: The Global Assault Continues" (www.wri.org/wri/wr-98-99/deforest.htm)

8.14　*SA 1993*, p. 230, Table 380. *SA 1994*, p. 237, Table 377. *SA 1998*, p. 247, Table 411. Note: Endangered defined as "in danger of becoming extinct throughout all or a significant part of its natural range." Text: *Time*, 6/30/97, p. 23. *World Press Review*, May 1997, p. 29.

8.15　*WR*, pp. 264-65, Table 8.5. Text: Robert J. Downing, Ramesh Ramankutty, and Jitendra Shah, *Rains-Asia: An Assessment Model for Acid Deposition in Asia* (Washington: World Bank 1997).

8.16　Carbon Dioxide Information Analysis Center, Oak Ridge National Laboratories, "Regional CO2 Emissions from Fossil-Fuel Burning, Cement Manufacture, and Gas Flaring, 1751-1996" (http://cdiac.esd.ornl.gov/ftp/ndp030/region96.ems). Text: *WR*, "Climate Brief: Searching for a Greenhouse Fingerprint" (www.wri.org/wri/wr-98-99/climate1.htm).

Chapter 9: Macroeconomics

9.1　*SCB* 78, no. 8, pp. 151-52, Table 2a. BEA, "National Accounts Data," Table 1 (www.bea.doc.gov/bea/dn/niptbl-d.htm).

9.2　*SCB* 78, no. 8, p. 163, Table 4. *ERP* 1999, p. 368, Table B-35.

9.3　*SCB* 78, no. 8, p. 151, Table 2A. BEA, "National Accounts Data" (www.bea.doc.gov/bea/dn/niptbl-d.htm).

9.5　*ERP 1999*, p. 385, Table B-50.

9.6　Capital Stock. Non-residential, non-financial capital stock valued at current cost. NIPA (www.stat-usa.gov/Online.nsf/vwFileLookup/7KCU.TXT/$File/7KCU.TXT?OpenElement). For non financial corporate profits: *NIPA 1929-82*, pp. 61-62, Table 1.16. *SCB 75*, no. 11/12, pp. 45-46, Table 8. SCB 77, no. 4, p. D-5, Table 1.16. *SCB 78*, no. 11, p. D-5, Table 1.16. *SCB 71*, no. 9, p. 6, Table 1.16. *SCB 72*, no. 9, p. 8, Table 1.16. SCB 73, no. 9, p. 10, Table 1.16. *SCB 74*, no. 9, p. 9, Table 1.16.

9.7　*ERP 1995*, p. 386, Table B-97. *SA 1998*, p. 553, Table 877. Text: *SA 1998*, p. 554, Table 879.

9.8　*SA 1998*, p. 556, Table 884. *SA 1995*, p. 555, Table 869.

9.9　*ERP 1999*, p. 412, Table B-73. GDP Deflator: *SCB 79*, no. 1, pp. D-36-38, Table C-1.

9.11　Federal Deposit Insurance Corporation, "1996 Historical Statistics on Banking" (www.fdic.gov/databank/hsob/cb01.html).

9.12　Board of Governors of the Federal Reserve System, *Flow of Funds Accounts: 1946-1997*, 8/11/98, Table F1.

9.13　*ERP* 1991, p. 393, Table B-93. *ERP* 1999, p. 436, Table B-95.

9.14　Board of Governors of the Federal Reserve System, *Flow of Funds Accounts*, Sept. 11, 1998. 1945-53, 1954-62, 1963-72, 1973-81, 1982-90, 1991-97, Tables F-100 (p. 8) and L-100 (p. 54). Text: "Personal bankruptcy filings by state" (www.bankrate.com/brm/news/pf/19980114a.asp), 1/14/98.

9.15　OECD, *Main Economic Indicators*, Nov. 1998, pp. 20-31.

9.16　*SCB* 78, no. 8, pp. 151-52, Table 1a.

Chapter 10: The Global Economy

10.1 Growth rates: *WDI* 1998, pp. 176-78, Table 4.1. Text: *WDI* 1998, pp. 24-26, Table 1.4.

10.2 OECD *Main Economic Indicators*, May 1999, pp. 208, 211. Text: Ulrich Beck, "Capitalism Without Work," *Dissent* (Winter 1997).

10.3 *SA 1994*, p. 551, Table 855. *SA 1997*, p. 550, Table 859.

10.4 *NIPA* 1929-1958, p. 19, Table 1.14; p. 24, Table 1.15. *NIPA* 1958-1988, Table 1.14 & 1.15. *SCB* 72, no. 7, p. 54, Table 1.14. *SCB* 74, no. 7, p. 59, Table 1.14. *SCB* 76, no. 8, p. 25, Table 1.14. *SCB* 78, no. 8, p. 45, Table 1.14.

10.5 UN, *World Economic and Social Survey 1998*, p. 141, Table A.16.

10.6 BLS News Release, "International Comparisons of Hourly Compensation Costs for Production Workers in Manufacturing, 1997," 9/17/98, Table 2 (http://stats.bls.gov/news/release/ichcc.toc.htm). *SA 1998*, pp. 801-04, Table 1323.

10.7 *The World's Women 1970-1990: Trends and Statistics* (New York: United Nations, 1991), pp. 104-05, Table 8. *The World's Women 1995: Trends and Statistics* (New York: United Nations, 1995), pp. 141-42, Table 11. International Monetary Fund, *International Financial Statistics Yearbook* (Washington: IMF, 1998).

10.8 UNCTAD, *World Investment Report 1998*, p. 59, Table III.5.

10.9 UNCTAD, *World Investment Report 1998* p. 5, Table I.3.

10.10 *WDI 1998*, p. 334, Table 6.8.

10.11 Bank for International Settlements, *Annual Report 1999*, Table V5 (www.bis.org/publ/ar99e6.pdf).

10.12 OECD *Main Economic Indicators*, Dec. 1998, p. 225.

10.13 UNCTAD, *World Investment Report 1998* p. 57, Table III.3.

10.14 Paul Krugman, "The Return of Depression Economics," *Foreign Affairs*, Jan/Feb 1999, p. 56. David Kotz, "Capitalist Collapse," *DS*, Nov/Dec 1998, pp. 10-11, 39. John Miller, "Learning from the Southeast Asian Crisis," *DS*, Nov/Dec. 1998, pp. 12-15, 40. *TE*, Feb 6-12, 1999, pp. 77-78; Feb 13-19, 1999, pp. 70-71.

10.15 IMF, *International Monetary Statsitics*, Aug. 1997 , pp. 361, 363; Nov. 1997, pp. 355, 357; May 1997, pp. 359, 361; Nov. 1998, pp. 365, 367; Feb. 1999, pp. 371, 373. Text: *Time International*, 11/23/98, p. 24.

10.16 UNICEF, *State of the World's Children 1999*, pp. 99-101, Table 2.

10.17 *HDR 1998*, pp. 2, 4, 50. Text: *HDR 1998*, pp. 6, 47, 50.

10.18 *WDI 1998*, p. 12, Table 1.1; p. 20, Table 1.3. Text: *WDI 1998*, p. 76, Table 2.10; p. 88, Table 2.13; p. 92, Table 2.14. *Monthly Labor Review* 110, no. 6 (June 1987), p. 104, Table 46. *Monthly Labor Review* 117, no. 9 (Sept 1994), pp. 118-19, Table 46-47.